A LIFE TOUCHED BY NATURE

Bermuda bound April 9, 1930.

A Biography of
JACK CONNERY

A Life Touched by Nature

PAUL BUTLER

A LIFE TOUCHED BY NATURE: A BIOGRAPHY OF JACK CONNERY

Copyright © 2022 by Paul Butler

Published by Little Red Hen Press.

All rights reserved. This book may not be reproduced in whole or in part, in any form (beyond copying permitted by Sections 107 and 108 of the United States Copyright Law, and except limited excerpts by reviewer for the public press), without written permission from Paul Butler. For permission, or to contact Paul Butler, please email casajard@gmail.com.

For a complete list of photo credits, please see *Picture Credits* at the end of the book.

Author services by Pedernales Publishing, LLC.
www.pedernalespublishing.com

Cover design: Paul Butler and Jose Ramirez

Library of Congress Control Number: 2022906887

ISBN 978-0-9979666-0-2 Hardcover Edition
ISBN 978-0-9979666-9-5 Paperback Edition

Printed in the United States of America

Contents

Preface ... 1

Chapter 1: Early Years in Savannah & Chattanooga ... 3

Chapter 2: Move to Florida & Becoming an Eagle Scout ... 9

Chapter 3: Making his Mark in Ornithology with Oscar Baynard ... 17

Chapter 4: An Encounter with William Beebe ... 26

Chapter 5: With Beebe in Bermuda ... 33

Chapter 6: Arrival of the Bathysphere ... 40

Chapter 7: Return to Florida & Rollins College ... 48

Chapter 8: Marriage & Mead Botanical Garden ... 64

Chapter 9: Difficult Times in the 1940s ... 80

Chapter 10: The Deland Years ... 93

Chapter 11: The African Violet Business ... 102

Chapter 12: Closure ... 112

Acknowledgments ... 118

Notes ... 120

Picture Credits ... 141

Preface

Mead Botanical Garden in Winter Park, Florida is where all this began. The year was early 2010 and I had just arrived from the UK as a new immigrant and plant-lover, keen to experience horticultural in Florida's semi-tropical climate, particularly where it included a plant I had always wished to cultivate, the orchid. About all I knew then of the Garden was that Edwin Grover, Professor of Books at Rollins College in Winter Park, and a young naturalist and Eagle Scout by the name of Jack Connery were the initial founders, and that when it opened in 1940 it was crammed full of Theodore Mead's beautiful prize orchids.

It was no surprise that there were no longer any of Mead's orchids in the Garden after a passage of seventy years, but I did wonder about the man the Garden was named after, Theodore Mead, one of America's foremost horticulturists and orchid specialists. I was struck by the absence of an authoritative written account of him, so with the help of letters and diaries and some photographs, I completed his biography, *Orchids & Butterflies*, in 2016.

In further researching the Mead Botanical Garden story, and how the Garden came about, I encountered considerable misinformation and plain incorrectness in much of the written material. I discovered a 1995 letter that Jack Connery's wife, Helen, had sent to the Winter Park library archivist there at the time, Donna

Rhein, in response to a request for information about Jack Connery and his involvement in the Garden. In the letter, Helen writes, "I had felt that someday someone would be puzzled by all the misconceptions and misinformation – and lack of knowledge – floating around concerning the Mead Garden." Like Helen I was equally annoyed with incorrect information, so I turned my attention to correctly documenting the history of the Garden, an exercise resulting in the second book, *Hope Springs Eternal*, published in 2019.

Edwin Grover and Jack Connery were the parents of Mead Botanical Garden. Both were enigmatic characters that, although opposites, worked together well as a team. Grover was the intellectual, the writer and the passionate and energetic promoter; Connery the organized and hard-working doer, with a strong desire to memorialize his mentor, Theodore Mead. In the early days of the Garden, both Jack and Helen Connery were tireless workers in the Garden, but they both left in the early 1950s when the City of Winter Park took it over.

Of the two founders, more is known about Grover and his achievements at Rollins College and in Mead Botanical Garden than Connery. Eduard Gfeller completed an excellent biography of Edwin Grover, published as *The Business of Making Good*, leaving Jack Connery's story the only one not yet told.

This volume then completes the trilogy of books on the man, Theodore Mead, the history of his Garden, and the life and times of its key visionary founder, Jack Connery.

Paul Butler
Henley-on-Thames
February 2022

CHAPTER 1

Early Years in Savannah & Chattanooga

Jack Connery was descended from an Irish Catholic immigrant family. His great grandfather, Charles H. Connery, was born in Dublin around 1815 and arrived in the United States through New York in 1834. The newly-arrived immigrant settled in the New Haven district of Connecticut where he married Louisa Hurd. The next record of him is in Savannah, Georgia in 1860 with a family of three sons, partnering with William Hone as a ship chandler, under the business name of Hone & Connery. The eldest son, Charles Pentland Connery, married Anna S. Hone a daughter of his father's business partner, and produced Jack's father, William Hone Connery, in 1881.

William Hone Connery's early working life was spent employed as a clerk in various Savannah wholesale and retail goods businesses, and as a youth, under the preferred name Hone Connery, he developed an interest and passion in bicycling and photography. The cycle craze hit America in the 1880s and took off as a popular activity with the Connery brothers. His elder brother, Charles Pentland Jr., was a bicycle mechanic, and became a well-known young amateur racer in

Savannah. Hone had a spell in 1897 as a clerk at the Savannah Cycle Agency on Bull Street, and started off as a trick cyclist, performing at race meetings between heats as additional entertainment, but eventually took up the racing side of the sport and won several competitions as a result.

Hone's interest in photography coincided with the period when Kodak released the popular Brownie camera that fostered the establishment of retail outlets selling cameras and film and offering developing and printing capabilities. Convinced that the photography business offered good career opportunities, he set about building a reputation in the Savannah area as an up-and-coming young photographer.

He was particularly intrigued by the photographic process of creating twin images that could be viewed in three-dimensions through the use of a stereoscope and, like most families, the Connerys had a large selection of stereoview cards depicting scenes from all over the world. Several large companies, such as Underwood & Underwood, H. C. White, Griffith & Griffith, and the Keystone View Company, became producers of the cards and were active commissioning photographers to collect images, sold generally in sets. Among the popular themes were views of the engineering marvels of the industrial age, such as the building of skyscrapers and the American railroads, and travelogue or sightseeing slides that showed the wonders of the National Parks or the pyramids and tombs of ancient Egypt.

In early 1902, the twenty-one-year-old Hone responded to a request from Griffith & Griffith for a photographer to visit Cuba in May of that year to record stereo views of the inauguration of Cuba's independence. As the time of his departure neared, a volcanic eruption on the island of Martinique occurred and this location together with a visit to San Juan, Porto Rico, were added to his commission itinerary. He would be gone for around two months and at such a young age was showing all the characteristic independence of spirit and desire for adventure that Jack would inherit.

Hone left Savannah on May 18, 1902 bound for Cuba and entered Havana harbor on the first ship flying the Cuban flag on May 20, the day of the inauguration of the

Cuban government. He photographed the independence celebrations in Havana before taking a Herrara Line steamer along the north coast of Cuba, stopping at all the ports along the way to take photographs, before calling at Santo Domingo in the Dominican Republic and ending at San Juan, in Porto Rico. He found the city charming, commenting "There is an American air about the city that makes you feel at home." He also noted that there was only one photographer in San Juan and as a result of the monopoly he was 'coining money'.

During the early months of May, the volcanic Mt. Pelée on Martinique, which he wanted to photograph as part of his commission, had erupted several times. The most violent event was on May 8 when a huge cloud of incandescent lava particles descended rapidly down the flank of the volcano obliterating the town of Saint-Pierre and killing almost the entire population of 30,000 people. Transportation between Porto Rico and Martinique was badly affected and a quarantine established for non-essential passengers meant that he was unable to visit the island and photograph the scenes of destruction. Instead, he returned to Havana and continued to document the city, countryside and remnants of the Spanish-American war, increasing the total number of pictures taken on the trip to over 600. He departed for New York on the Ward Line, and after going through quarantine, went to Griffith & Griffith in Philadelphia to develop his plates, arriving back in Savannah in late July. A full description of his trip appeared in the local newspaper.

For many years, as part of the normal social interactions in Savannah society, the Connery family had got to know the Englerth family, who lived a few city-blocks away. They were regular visitors to each other's homes. Hone got to know the many Englerth sisters and youngest son Basley, showing all the sisters varying degrees of affection, but he was particularly attracted to the middle sister, Viola.

1.1: Top: At the turn of the century, providing entertainment and education in most middle-class drawing rooms was the hand-held stereoscope and collections of card-mounted stereoviews, the first mass-produced photographs. Bottom: One of Hone Connery's 1902 views for Griffith & Griffith of the Cabanas Fortress from Morro Castle, Havana.

William Hone Connery married Viola Clarissa Englerth on December 22, 1902, at the home of her parents at 518 E. Waldburg Street. Two of her younger sisters, Nilla (Tenilla) on mandolin, and Addie on guitar, played Wagner's Lohengrin wedding march as the bride entered the room, wearing a gown of white silk tissue with lace and carrying white carnations. Another sister, Rita, attended her as maid of honor. The best man was Henry Thompson, originally from Jacksonville, a close friend and cycling companion and occasional competitor on the track of the two Connery brothers.

After the ceremony, the couple left by sea for New York, then after a short stay sailed for San Juan, Porto Rico. The city and its photographic opportunities had made a big impression on him months before and he had negotiated a position in San Juan as general manager of an American photographic supply company, most likely Kodak. Their first son, William Hone Connery Jr., was born there in 1904.

A move to Chattanooga in Tennessee followed in 1905 when he secured a managerial position in the photography department of T. H. Payne at 823 Market Street, one of Chattanooga's oldest businesses established in 1865 as a book and stationery store. The family grew with the birth of their second son, Thomas Andrew Connery, in 1905. Hone stayed with T. H. Payne until 1910 when, aged twenty-nine, he moved to become manager of the Kodak department at Harris & Hogshead. In 1911, he held the position of Kodak finisher – responsible for developing, printing and framing – at Austin Photo Supply Co. on Cherry Street in Chattanooga. By 1916, he had his own business, Connery Photo Supply Co., at 111 E. 8th Street. His brother-in-law, William Basley Englerth, moved from Savannah to Chattanooga to join him as a partner, becoming secretary/treasurer in the new business venture.

In the intervening years, Hone and Viola enlarged their family further producing John Hurd Connery on October 23, 1908; Charles Joseph Connery in 1911; a daughter, Thelma Viola Connery in 1915; and the final member of the family, Charles Pentland Connery, in December 1919. It appears that there was a minor parental disagreement over John Hurd Connery's first names, because his official birth certificate records him as Jack R., and Jack is what he always called himself and was commonly known as to family and friends throughout his life. The name John H. appears on some census documents, including the 1910 Federal census when he was two years old, but it is Jack or Jack H. on others. It wasn't until 1947 that a correction by affidavit was made to the certificate and Jack R. crossed out and John Hurd written in, presumably just before he secured his passport to go to Cuba.

1.2: Jack Connery's legal birth certificate, indicating the name "Jack R." and the alteration by affidavit on October 23, 1947 to "John Hurd".

Chapter 2

Move to Florida & Becoming an Eagle Scout

The cold Tennessee winters were not to Hone's liking, and in October 1919 he travelled to Florida to investigate photographic business opportunities, first to St. Petersburg, and then Orlando, which he preferred. He was taken by a little Orlando cottage with land and a large outbuilding at 727 W. Colonial Drive, and in March 1920 he bought the 1.2-acre plot and moved his family there. The outbuilding in the grounds of the property was converted into the Orlando Photo Studio and workshop, with sleeping quarters for the Connery sons upstairs. Hone had a telephone installed between the cottage and the workshop so Viola knew how many to expect for breakfast in the mornings.

Meanwhile the Connery Photo Supply company in Tennessee, left under his brother-in-law's care, needed Hone's attention and he made several trips to Chattanooga to assist in managing the business. On one of the trips, he purchased and mailed back to Jack a fishing rod and reel that had the teenager over the moon. Viola wrote back to Hone telling him of Jack's delight at receiving the gift and that "you never saw a child more so than he was when he opened the package." The Chattanooga business was eventually sold to Basley, who renamed it Englerth's Camera Shop and developed it into a successful photographic business. He relocated the store to 722 Cherry Street in 1933 and it became the standard provider of portrait and school yearbook photographs throughout the 1930s and beyond.

In 1926 the Connerys added a much larger two-story Dutch colonial style house to the plot which extended around the corner to the original cottage, renumbered 719 Hayden Lane. The new larger residence and studio were renumbered as 741 W. Colonial Drive, and with its large garden became the hub for family activities and gatherings. Business was brisk at the Orlando Photo Studio that stressed its thirty-year experience as a Kodak finishing business in advertisements in the local newspaper.

2.1: A 1927 Orlando Sentinel newspaper advertisement for the Connery's Orlando Photo Studio at 741 W. Colonial Drive.

As teenagers, and under Hone's tutelage, all the Connery children gained photographic experience in camera use, studio lighting, and the process of developing, printing and framing photographs. Four of the five brothers, Bill, Tom, Joe and Charlie, followed in their father's footsteps working in the family business as portrait photographers and finishers, until eventually becoming photographers in their own right. Thelma's first husband, Bill Reynolds, was a photographer too and she became skilled in the developing and tinting of printed personalized Christmas cards, frequently showing the front of the client's residence. Jack also played his part through his teenage years working in the studio part-time and in 1929, aged twenty, he spent a full year after leaving school working as a photographic finisher.

But Jack's long-term calling was a little different from that of his siblings. As a young teenager, like his father before him, he yearned for the excitement of seeing and seeking adventure in the natural world, and was keen to learn new skills and take on new challenges. An organization which allowed him to explore these desires came about shortly after the family arrived in Orlando, when the Boy Scouts of America organized a Central Florida Council charged with implementing a quality scouting program to all youth in this geographical area. A call for boys between the ages of twelve to seventeen was sent out and as soon as possible after Jack's twelfth birthday he signed up and became a member of Troop 5, Orlando, under the leadership of Scoutmaster Oscar Edward Baynard, an experienced scoutmaster and deputy commission for the Central Florida Council. He was also a renowned naturalist and bird expert, a well-known photographer of birds and their nests and eggs, and one of the unsung heroes of the Audubon cause in Florida. His influence on Jack would be profound.

Jack threw himself into the scouting culture, putting himself forward for team leadership challenges at every opportunity and rapidly acquired merit badges. On October 26, 1923 at the Scout Headquarters in Orlando, he was awarded merit badges in Bird Study, Carpentry, Cooking, Firemanship, Lifesaving, and

Painting. Also at the meeting, Carl Dann Jr., who would later join Jack in his ornithological adventures, advanced to the rank of second class. More merit badges followed for Jack leading to the award in November 1923 of Life and Star badges and finally with twenty-one merit badges to his credit, the coveted award of Eagle Scout in February, 1924. He would become only the third scout in Central Florida to receive this honor.

2.2: Left: Oscar Baynard, Jack's first scoutmaster and ornithologist, photographed in 1911. Right: In 1924, Jack became one of the first scouts in Central Florida to receive the Eagle Scout Badge.

Summer camp was a highlight of the scouting year, initially held at the Silver Lake site, near Sanford. In 1922, in a pivotal moment of his life, he met his future horticultural mentor there, Theodore Mead, scoutmaster of the Oviedo troop. Instructive talks by invited guests were a feature of camp life and Mead was a popular visitor that year, energetically leading campfire singing and story-telling.

As a result of this meeting, Jack visited Mead at Oviedo and was shown his greenhouse full of prize orchids and all his other semi-tropical plants.

Also popular at the summer camps were swimming contests, boxing matches, and games, with healthy rivalry between the different troops. When the camp was over, there were additional Scout Rally days throughout the year offering friendly competition, and in 1924 at the Fair Grounds in Orlando, Jack won the fire by friction contest by generating fire in a time of thirty seconds.

Camping at Silver Lake continued until 1925, when the Central Florida Council of the Boy Scouts of America bought a forty-acre plot with four lakes near Plymouth, Florida and established Camp Wewa, meaning the camp of many waters, as their own permanent site. Many Orlando businesses contributed money and materials to build the necessary camp facilities and donated radio equipment and four boats and a canoe for water sports. Jack was introduced to sailing and boating at a young age and was always comfortable on the water and around boats.

2.3: *Jack was never happier than when out on the water in a boat.*

As well as boating, swimming was a major recreational activity at the camps and this was reflected in their new motto, "every scout a swimmer". With his lifesaving award, Jack frequently assisted in teaching the few boys who couldn't swim how to swim, and as an Eagle Scout joined the panel of expert examiners tasked with assessing the boys on their work for merit badges. The camp opened on August 1, 1925, and ran for four weeks and could accommodate around 100 scouts.

On one afternoon the scouts were entertained by a bird talk from Dr. William F. Blackman, ex-president of Rollins College and current president of the Florida Audubon Society. Suitably inspired, the Eagle scouts decided to create a new trail at the site to encourage bird study, erecting bird bungalows, feed tables and bird baths along the trail. By the beginning of 1926, many other improvements to the site had been made, and the camp facilities had been upgraded; tents had been replaced by screened timber cabins and an office quarters and circular mess hall with a concrete floor had been built, resulting in the camp now being described as a Boy Scouts Paradise.

2.4: *Jack was a member of the Orlando High School golf team in 1928, captained by Carl Dann, Jr.*

Carl Dann Jr. was a scout member of Troop 1, Orlando and a school friend of Jack's at Orlando High School. His father, Carl Dann Sr., was a Central Florida property developer who created the Dubsdread golf course in Orlando that opened in 1924. As a result, the young Dann had golf in his blood and captained the Orlando High School's golf team as a senior in 1928 with Jack as a player member of that year's team.

2.5: The scene at Daytona Beach on March 11, 1929, when Major Henry Segrave broke the world land-speed record travelling at 231.45 mph. Jack's camera shutter recorded just the blur as the Golden Arrow sped past.

Jack left Orlando High School in 1928 and spent 1929 working in the family photographic studio and, in his spare time, adding to his ornithological collection. An opportunity for excitement came in March when it was announced that Henry Segrave, in his high-speed racer Golden Arrow, would make an attempt on the land speed record at nearby Daytona Beach. Jack was there at that event and managed to capture one of Segrave's record-breaking runs as the massive gold-colored car sped down the course in the presence of thousands of spectators who lined the entire nine-miles of dunes bordering the measured mile. Segrave's speed was a world record-breaking 231.45 mph.

Now, at the age of twenty, Jack had developed a strong attraction to the natural world, much of it inspired by and channeled through the scouting movement. He would stay active as a scout all his life, eventually becoming scoutmaster of Troop 59, Winter Park in 1938. Jack would never forget the influence that two older more experienced scoutmasters had on his appreciation of nature's bounty. The first was Theodore Mead, scoutmaster of the Oviedo troop, who introduced him to the world of plants, the other, Oscar Baynard, his original scoutmaster in 1921, who introduced him to the world of birds.

Chapter 3

Making his Mark in Ornithology with Oscar Baynard

Oscar Baynard came to Florida from Delaware in 1903, and initially settled in Micanopy, south of Gainesville. Already an accomplished ornithologist, he became curator of the nearby Florida State Museum. He was an early subscriber to the Florida Audubon Society, established in the lakeside Maitland home of Clara and Louis Dommerich in March 1900. This founding meeting took place with influential members of the local community, many connected with Rollins College, including William Blackman, the college's fourth president. The founder's overarching concern was the protection of Florida's unique bird species, particularly those like the snowy egret that were been hunted and killed remorselessly for their showy feathers to supply plumes for ladies' hats. Despite the introduction of protective laws to prevent the killing of birds for their feathers, the practice was still common in rural Florida. The society hoped that by identifying bird sanctuaries and assigning an Audubon warden to patrol them the process could be halted.

3.1: Bird Island, in the distance, was a thirty-six-acre floating island in Orange Lake, Alachua County, Florida that was home to thousands of nesting egrets, ibis and herons.

In 1910, Baynard had identified a suitable site near his home in Micanopy that needed protection from the plume hunters. Bird Island, as it became known, was a large floating island of around thirty-six acres in Orange Lake, Alachua County, about one mile from the landing at Orange Lake Station. Baynard had got to know the island and was a regular visitor. It was the breeding place of thousands of pairs of ibis, egrets, and heron and he believed it was one of the most richly populated rookeries in Florida and therefore a highly likely future target for the hunters. He proposed that the National Association of Florida Societies purchase the island and appoint him warden, which they agreed to do. His tenure was successful but short, from 1911 to 1914, when he handed the job over to an equally effective and well-qualified Audubon warden. This success story led him to claim that "There are probably more egrets in Alachua County than in all the rest of the State and with the vigorous protection that they are now receiving here, it is hoped that they may be the means of repopulating the State with this showy and valuable bird."

Baynard spent Christmas 1912 cruising among the keys of the Gulf coast, from Clearwater to Cortez, identifying and photographing birds and accompanied by William Blackman, who by then was the president of the Florida Audubon Society. They identified about forty species which they listed for publication in *Bird Lore*, the Society's inhouse publication, as their contribution to the traditional Christmas Day inventory of bird species seen on that day. Blackman joined Baynard on many ornithology expeditions. On one occasion in 1915, in the process of exploring bald eagle nesting sites, Baynard climbed a tall pine tree and brought two eaglets down to show Blackman, before reclimbing the tree to put them back in their nest.

3.2: *William Blackman, President of the Florida Audubon Society, with two young bald eaglets in his hands, brought down to show Blackman by Oscar Baynard before he reclimbed the tree behind Blackman to put them back in their nest.*

Baynard moved to Orlando in the early 1920s to help with the scouting council's expansion plans for Central Florida, securing employment as superintendent with the McCormick-Hannah Lumber Company, and renting accommodation almost opposite the Connerys at 742 W. Colonial Drive. By now he had become a noted expert in photographing Florida's birds and their nests and eggs, being one of the few owning a state license for the collection of eggs, and was widely trusted in the accurate identification of his subjects.

Baynard taught Jack how to identify birds and their nests and eggs as part of a necessary step towards Jack's bird study scout merit badge, and shared an article he had written for the *Oologist* magazine on how best to photograph nests with eggs. One trick he shared was the use of a canoe for egg hunting around the edges of mangrove swamps, where the nests of some bird species were loosely woven and it was possible to see through from below and determine whether they contained eggs or not. They went egg-hunting together and, in April 1925, Jack took a photograph of a clutch of twelve eggs of the Florida Bobwhite, a type of quail, that was later used as an illustration in a scientific publication.

Jack became an Audubon Society member, one of Florida's youngest ornithologists, and obtained his license to legally collect eggs for scientific study. Baynard reminded him of the protocol of egg collecting now he had his permit: collect the absolute minimum and try to remove early in the laying season, when the female would invariably lay a second time. Sometimes the eggs he collected were close to hatching and promptly did so when he returned home. Jack became skilled at rearing the few that hatched this way and in due course returning the young birds to the wild.

3.3: Left: A nest containing a clutch of Bobwhite eggs photographed by Jack Connery on April 25, 1925. Right: Jack and some hatched chicks, circa 1924; note his Eagle Scout badge.

Baynard had never forgotten his first rookery experience to Bird Island and was determined to share it with his young protégé, now his neighbor. So sometime in the mid-1920s, he suggested to Jack that they visit an egret rookery he knew down on the Kissimmee prairie. Years later, Jack recounted this memorable event to a local newspaper, who published his impressions in a piece entitled "Jack Connery finds real adventure in rookery of egrets."

The first thing he recalled was the initial difficulty in reaching the rookery: "From the edge of the marsh where we entered, it was about five to six miles over to the rookery, which covered several acres of myrtle hammock land. Three miles of this distance made wading and swimming necessary, for part of that we were in water up to our armpits and part of the time the water was very deep and we had to carry cameras and other supplies on our head to keep them dry." Their reward as they approached the island was a deafening squawking of warning and a mass eruption of egrets into the air. In the rookery, they saw hundreds of nests each containing from three to five bluish-green eggs which looked, according to Jack, "like opaque gems arranged in a fairytale setting." They remained under cover for a while until the birds returned to their nests when they were able to photograph and study them more closely. They stayed there for about an hour and when they departed the film in their cameras had captured the day's experience, but not their feelings, which Jack summed up as being 'lost in wonderment'.

3.4: A brown pelican rookery photographed by Jack Connery.

The Florida bird that Oscar Baynard thought the most unsatisfactory from an oologist point of view, yet offered the greatest excitement and thrill, was the bald eagle. The thrill came from climbing a pine tree perhaps a hundred feet tall with a nest at the top; the disappointment from finding it empty of eggs when you got there. A tall pine tree with a nest at the top meant nothing since eagles reuse their nests and rarely build new ones. Baynard was a skilled tree climber and would typically climb up to twenty to thirty eagle nests every season, only a few times finding a clutch of eggs. Later in life he reckoned he had climbed over a thousand trees, mainly pine trees, in search of eagle eggs. He liked to tell the true story of how one Christmas Eve in 1910, he had climbed a 125-foot-tall pine tree on Merritt Island to an eagle's nest and decided to bivouac just below the nest to await the adult bird's return. He had the photographs to prove it, taken from the base of the tree by colleague Dr. R. H. Mills, and the experience documented in an article he wrote in the *Oologist*. When asked why he'd done such a thing, he replied "Just for the fun of it."

You needed a team to go eagle egg hunting and there were older scouts and other colleagues who were interested in sharing the adventure with Jack. It was a winter activity in areas where there were tall pine trees and little commercial development, and Baynard recommended Merritt Island as a good spot. Jack always had his camera with him, and on some of the expeditions, the company of Carl Dann Jr. and Joseph Howell Jr., Orlando scout naturalists also interested in bird study. Dann became a Rollins graduate, a Florida Audubon Society member, and turned out to be particularly strong, fearless and skillful when it came to wearing tree-climbing irons and scaling tall pine trees in search of eagle eggs. Joe Howell Jr. was three years younger than Jack and Carl, and eventually became a scout leader of the Winter Park Pathfinder Troop. He was also a Florida Audubon member, a Rollins graduate (class of '35), and a keen ornithologist, developing a particular interest in the nesting habits of the Florida bald eagle. He was a tree climber too but learned the hard way – falling out of a large pine tree on an eagle egg collecting outing at the age of fifteen in December 1928 and spraining both ankles and his back.

3.5: December was eagle egg collecting time among the tall longleaf pines of Merritt Island. When a suitable candidate with a nest was identified (top left), one of the team wearing tree-climbing irons scaled the tree to reach it (top right). If the nest had eggs, there would be generally just two (bottom). The person at the top of the tree by the nest and in the lower image holding the eagle eggs is believed to be Carl Dann Jr.

Jack, Carl and Joe, together with more senior members of the various scout troops, took trips out to Merritt Island in the late 1920s and early 1930s during the key eagle egg-laying month of December. The results of successful trips were generally captured on Jack's camera.

Oscar Baynard moved to Plant City, Florida, in the late 1920s and became a poultry farmer, operating the Baywood Poultry Farm on Knights Road, where he had a hatchery and produced and sold eggs and baby chicks. He carefully examined the economics of egg production for various chicken breeds, ending up preferring the Ancona over the White Leghorn. He remained a lifelong scouter and was scoutmaster to the established all-Eagle Scout Plant City troop 5, and was awarded the scoutmasters key in 1934, the highest award a volunteer scouter could achieve. In the mid-1930s, he held various positions at Highlands Hammock State Park as a naturalist and guide, and contributed to the Christmas Day tradition of listing every bird species found in the 1,280 acres of the park. On that day in 1937, he identified eighty-four species, including the rare ivory-billed woodpecker. In 1936 he was appointed the first superintendent of Hillsborough State Park, a position he held until 1947. He had a 1,500-egg collection containing samples of over 700 different species of birds, all natives to the eastern seaboard of the US, and in 1959 he donated it to the St. Petersburg Historical Museum. The reason for the donation, he said, was "It's hard to find a place to put them all at home."

Jack never lost his keen interest in the study of birds, once remarking that "Bird life is the most fascinating and instructive of all nature studies, and gives the greatest satisfaction in results, for the reason that we find birds that sing, some that swim and dive, and others which walk, or fly or talk."

Chapter 4

An Encounter with William Beebe

Scouting was great fun, especially camping in the wilderness, as was hunting the countryside for bird eggs and nests to add to his ornithological collection, but Jack's canvas was broad and he yearned for a global nature adventure, the more exotic the better. In 1920s America, no one was more popular than Dr. William Beebe in epitomizing the genre of the naturalist world adventurer.

4.1: *William Beebe at his desk in his studio at the New York Zoological Society on West 67th Street, New York City.*

Beebe's background in ornithology secured an appointment in 1899 as Assistant Curator of Birds at the New York Zoological Park (now the Bronx Zoo), an institution founded by the New York Zoological Society. This led to a position as Curator of Birds in 1902, and then Director of the newly created Department of Tropical Research in 1916. Always active, and travelling the world to bring back specimens for the Zoo, he had explored the bird life of Mexico and British Guiana, circumnavigated the world documenting pheasants, investigated marine life in the Sargasso Sea, and studied the diversity of animal life on the Galapagos Islands, all before he was forty. He was a prolific author and produced articles and photographic accounts of his expeditions that were published in book form and in popular newspapers and magazines. He had a gift for making descriptions of his travels exciting and appealing to the general reader without compromising their scientific value. His books became best-sellers and people avidly followed his adventures and wondered what on earth the swashbuckling celebrity naturalist would do next.

4.2: *Jack attended a Sorosis meeting in Orlando in 1925 and heard extracts from William Beebe's latest book,* Galapagos: World's End; *an experience that motivated him to try to join Beebe on one of his expeditions.*

In early December 1925, aged sixteen, Jack had been taken by his mother to a meeting at Sorosis House on Liberty Street, Orlando to hear Mrs. C. O. Standish describe and read from William Beebe's latest book, *Galapagos: World's End*. Impressed by what he heard, and realizing that this was the kind of natural world adventure he was looking for, Jack vowed that someday he would try to join Beebe on one of his expeditions.

On a visit to New York in late September 1926, he made contact with Beebe in his laboratory at the New York Zoological Park, and spent the day examining the collection of birds Beebe had brought back from British Guiana as part of his study of bird life. He then returned to Florida to concentrate on his ornithology and complete his schooling.

Throughout the second half of the 1920s, Beebe moved the focus of his work on his annual expeditions away from ornithology to ecology and marine biology. In his visits to the Sargasso Sea, and a return trip to the Galapagos in 1925, he started to study marine life by net collecting sea creatures at varying oceanic depths. He also descended to the seabed in shallow water wearing a protective helmet fed with air via an umbilical hose, so he could observe sea creatures in their native habitat. Much new information about sea life was obtained this way.

In 1929, in what was the twelfth expedition of the Department of Tropical Research of the New York Zoological Society, he repeated the techniques of marine study around Nonsuch Island off the coast of Bermuda. He trawled for creatures using silk nets and shared the helmet diving sessions with members of his team to allow them to directly experience the amazing spectacle of undersea life.

4.3: *In the late 1920s, before the age of scuba diving, helmet diving with surface-supplied air allowed underwater exploration down to about 60 feet. Beebe embraced this technique for the direct scientific study of marine life at shallow depths.*

But for all his successes, Beebe remained dissatisfied with his progress in marine biology. Net-caught creatures were a random lottery and some caught in nets from the deepest part of the ocean and brought to the surface were mutilated beyond scientific study by the resultant change in pressure. Helmet diving, although exciting and interesting, was only feasible down to about 10 fathoms or 60 feet. Beebe wanted to go deeper and directly observe marine life in the black unchartered depths of the ocean where he suspected many unknown species might be living.

Deep diving became his new obsession and he made no secret of the fact in the popular press that he wanted to explore the deepest parts of the ocean, which he believed would be teeming with unimaginable forms of life. He spent much time over the winter at his desk in the New York Zoological Park researching the various ways that had been used in the past to explore deep waters, and concluded that some sort of submersible would be needed. It would have to be capable of resisting the tremendous pressure exerted by the weight of water above the vessel, which doubled every thirty-three feet of depth and at a half-mile down was over half a ton per square inch.

Unknown to Beebe but just across town was a Harvard engineering graduate, Otis Barton, with a passion for the natural world and a similar desire to explore new life in the deep. He had designed a steel sphere as the optimum pressure vessel, with an entry/exit hatch and small viewing windows. It would have its own internal air supply and be tethered by a strong steel cable and communication links to the mother ship above. A fortuitous meeting took place in Beebe's office in early 1929 where Barton shared his proposed design and, although at first dismissive, Beebe came round to agreeing that the design was workable and the two should join together in deep ocean exploration. This decision was aided greatly by Barton's offer to build the device using his own funds. Implicit in the agreement was that Barton would accompany Beebe on the dives, which was not entirely to Beebe's egotistical liking but was a price he was willing to pay to achieve his dream.

Throughout 1929, Barton worked on the design and production of the underwater submersible, overseeing the initial casting of a steel sphere that was initially too heavy and had to be broken up and melted down for a second smaller and lighter one. The device was to have three three-inch-thick porthole windows made of fused quartz and was four feet nine inches in diameter, so the interior of the sphere was a squeeze for two adults. The spartan interior contained only a light and telephone, oxygen tanks, and trays of chemicals – soda lime to absorb carbon dioxide and calcium chloride to absorb moisture. The occupants would use hand-held palm tree fans, bought at the market in Bermuda, to circulate the air inside. Meanwhile Beebe had invented a name for the device – the bathysphere, from the Greek *bathus* meaning deep.

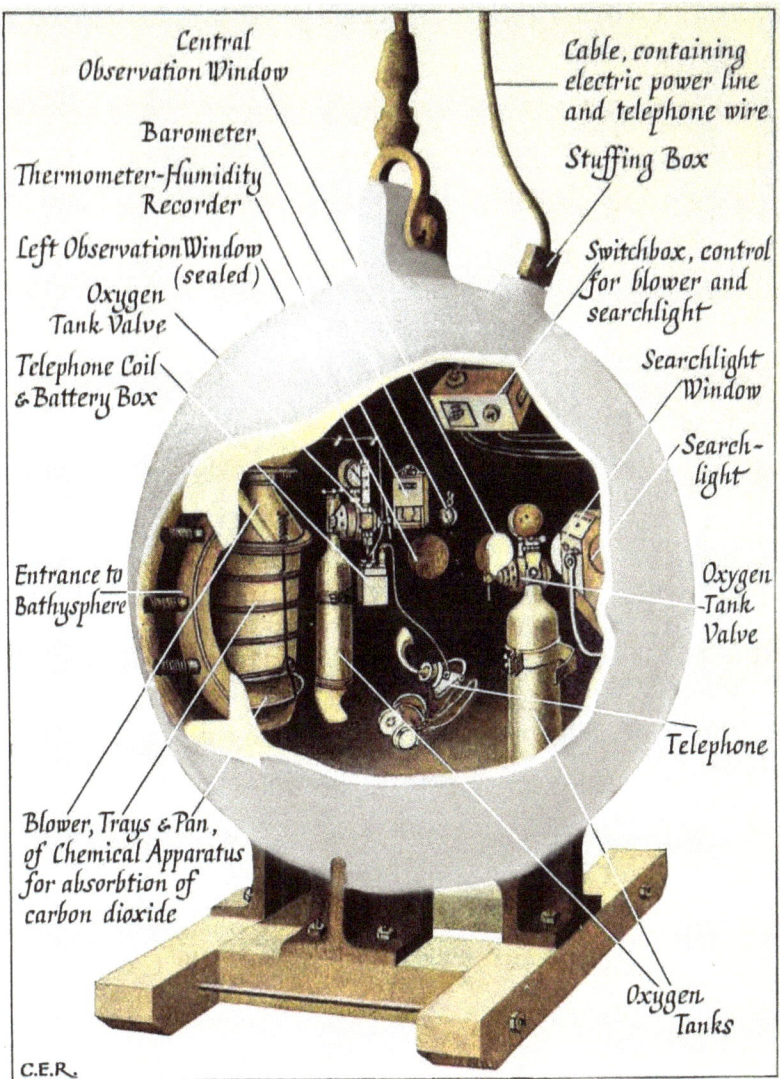

4.4: Detailed illustration of the Bathysphere and its interior. The viewing ports are directly opposite the fourteen-inch diameter entry/exit hatch.

In late 1929, when Jack heard the news that Beebe was planning an expedition to Bermuda to descend into the deep ocean in a steel sphere, he felt he had to act. So seizing the opportunity, in early 1930 he went to New York to renew the acquaintance he had first made some three years before and ask him whether he could join the expedition. Beebe was a charismatic and enthusiastic character who traditionally took along five or six young volunteer field assistants on his expeditions, hoping to infect them with his own naturalist's zeal. He interviewed each young potential team member, looking for knowledge, energy and infectious enthusiasm. On this occasion, Jack must have fitted the bill with his passion for ornithology and the natural world, his achievements as an Eagle Scout, and his camera and photographic darkroom expertise.

Jack spoke of the meeting several years later, confirming that it was his camera and photographic experience which resulted in him being accepted as the photographer's assistant for the expedition. He also recalled the surprise he felt when they arrived in Bermuda and found out he was the only photographer in the crew.

The bathysphere would be ready for the 1930 season when Beebe would return to Bermuda and Nonsuch Island, close to the point where the ocean floor descended to over two miles in depth. At that point, he and Barton would attempt to descend deeper into the ocean than anyone previously had, and Jack Connery would be there to photograph the event.

Chapter 5

With Beebe in Bermuda

The group selected for the 1930 Bermuda Oceanographic Expedition was made up of experienced participants of his previous expeditions, other experts and staff members from the New York Zoological Society, plus his normal sprinkling of college-educated young assistants. Joining Beebe in the advance party and essential to setting up the expedition facilities, laboratory and associated equipment, was general manager John Tee-Van, Beebe's right-hand man. Also in the group were Gloria Hollister, technical associate, Howard Barnes, zoologist, Llewellyn Miller, wildlife artist, Philbrick Crouch, electrical handyman, Margaret Elliott, laboratory assistant, Virginia Zeigler, secretary, and Jack Connery, photographer.

This group, together with Mrs. Beebe and Gloria's mother Elaine, left New York on the SS *Fort St. George* on April 9, 1930, arriving three days later in the town of St. George, Bermuda. Joining them a little later, once things were up and running, would be two more artists, Helen Tee-Van and Else Bostelmann, who would produce illustrations in color of the various marine life. Four more young field assistants, John Cannon, Jackson Guernsey, Patten Jackson, and Perkins Bass were expected shortly, and over the summer staff specialists William Gregory and Newton Harvey would arrive to help identify the ocean discoveries.

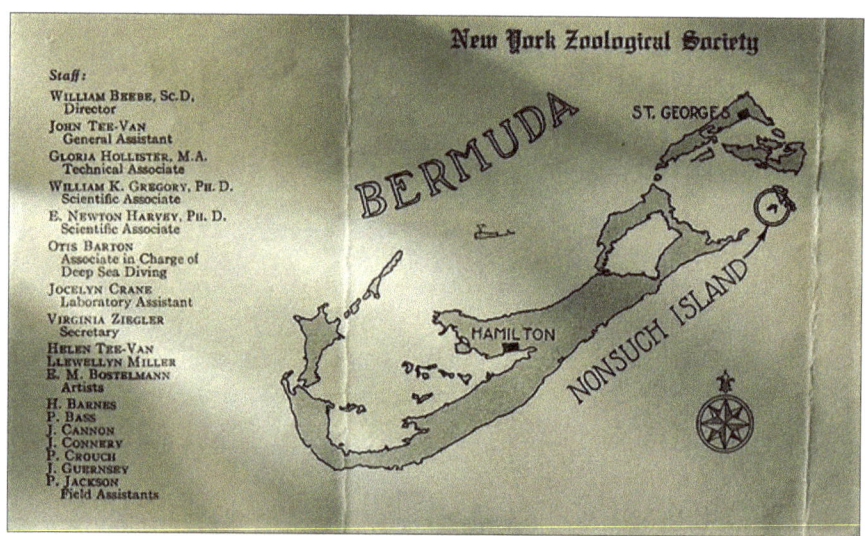

5.1: *Letterhead for the thirteenth expedition of the New York Zoological Society's Department of Tropical Research, listing the 1930 personnel and showing the position of their base off Bermuda on Nonsuch Island.*

5.2: *On board the SS* Fort St. George *en route to Bermuda. Left to right: Howard Barnes, Philbrick Crouch, William Beebe, Margaret Elliott, Virginia Zeigler, Gloria Hollister and her mother, Elaine. In front of Beebe is Gloria's dog, Trumps.*

After disembarking from the ship at Bermuda, they boarded a tender to the city wharf, where the party split up with senior staff going to the St. George Hotel. Tee-Van and the rest took boats through Castle Harbor to their research base on the island of Nonsuch, four miles southeast of St. George. Nonsuch was a small island of a few acres with a collection of buildings that were a yellow fever quarantine hospital many years before. The only island residents were a Bermuda government caretaker, Arthur Tucker, and his wife who was to be cook for the party. The old hospital would become the laboratory and the wards sleeping quarters for the staff. On the ridge plateau close to the main building were a series of white tents where the students were billeted with Jack in nominal charge, a position which suited him with his scouting background. It took two weeks of preparation to set up the laboratory before any deep-sea research using net trawling could begin. Beebe hired the sea-going tug *Gladisfen* and its Bermudian crew of five for net trawling, and Arthur Hollis, another Bermudian, assisted the team in general duties both at sea and in the laboratory.

5.3: Nonsuch Island from the air. The white building was a yellow fever quarantine hospital in the nineteenth century before being abandoned and subsequently leased to the New York Zoological Society for use as a marine research station.

Beebe's research strategy was to investigate marine life in a concentrated area several miles across and as deep as two miles. He wanted to identify the number and type of creatures as a function of depth, and study how their morphology and habits varied in response to the changes in the amount and color of light available. Shoreline trawling and helmet diving would give that data for the shallows and net trawling and dredging for the mid and deep ocean. Finally, the bathysphere would be used to directly observe the deeper regions and correlate what they saw with what was retrieved in the nets.

When Jack was on sea duty, a typical day began as an early seven o'clock start with Beebe, Tee-Vann and two or three of the other students descending to the wharf carrying racks of mason jars, pails, and extra nets. There Beebe's twenty-six-foot power launch *Skink* was waiting to take them out to the *Gladisfen*. The tug would run out five miles from shore to an imaginary cylinder estimated to be eight miles in diameter, where the water was from one to three miles deep, and a strong steel cable with a lead weight on the end let out to which were affixed a series of nets at hundred-fathom intervals along the cable. A further one mile of cable was then released which allowed the nets to be trolled in water a mile to one and one-half miles deep. The nets were made from the finest mesh silk to trap even the smallest examples of marine life. These nets were also used to investigate the marine population of shallow water close to shore where the nets were pulled in by hand.

After several hours of trawling, the cable was slowly reeled in and the nets detached in order of depth and their contents collected and washed and roughly sorted, with things of interest placed in quart jars and large living fish in a pail with ice. Notable to Jack were the many forms of life which produced "a most peculiar light, both when in and out of the water, and was very brilliant especially when taken and examined in the dark room of the photography laboratory." This observation of the marine phenomenon of bioluminescence, common in deep-sea creatures, would stay with him as one of the most astonishing experiences of the natural world.

Beebe had pioneered the use of helmet diving to study marine life. The shallow waters of Castle Harbor and its environs, with its many dark mysterious-shaped coral reefs set in exquisite ultramarine water and teeming with fish, was an ideal place to practice it safely. Beebe encouraged any visitors or members of the team who wanted to dive to do so. Scientific associate William Gregory had arrived in July with his protégé Jocelyn Crane, and Beebe took them both helmet diving off Gurnet Rock. Gregory stayed a month while Crane became an established member of Beebe's team.

5.4: *Top L: The trawling crew letting out the series of silk nets from the stern of the tugboat Gladisfen. Top R: A large marine species caught from the depths using dredging. Bottom: Shoreline net trawling by hand in the shallows of Tucker's Town Bay.*

Jack also took full advantage of helmet diving opportunities, as he stated later: "I have been under water many times, walking on the ocean floor at a depth of forty-five feet as easily as I would walk on this floor." He used the sixty-pound diving helmet, wore a bathing suit and had sneakers on his feet to protect them as he moved about over the sand.

When he took his first dive and stepped off the last rung of the ladder and floated slowly to the ocean floor, Jack described it as if entering an alien world of magnificent and weird architecture. Long dark shadows revealed themselves to be rocky cliffs of coral, resembling mosques with minarets topped with irregular jagged turrets. Looking about, he seemed to be able to see an indefinite distance as there was no horizon and far away everything just faded into nothingness. The sun's rays filtering down through the water produced a scene that was a myriad of shades and hues, and colored fish of many kinds and sizes swam around him and among the towering pinnacles of coral. Jack summed it up as, "I would never miss an opportunity to walk upon the ocean floor; for the thrilling experience is unlike anything else I can imagine." On his return to the surface, Beebe welcomed him as a fellow helmet diver into the 'Kingdom of the Helmet' and a member of the 'Society of Wonderers'.

Beebe worked hard and expected his crew to do the same. His team spent endless hours examining specimens and recording results, but Beebe was watchful over morale and on most evenings, he insisted on a ritual cocktail hour. Sometimes they attended formal parties with dancing at the St. George Hotel, but if Beebe sensed any serious flagging, he would declare it was his birthday in a few days even though it really wasn't, and there was going to be a costume party. It was a special occasion on his real birthday on July 29, when everyone dressed up in ragged outfits as pirates, some carrying knives and others smeared with fake blood. After cocktails and a good dinner, the party group ended up in the dungeon of the old castle on Castle Island which was lit with candles and lined with fish nets, and where they ate cake and drank beer and wine as a conclusion to the celebration.

When they could, Beebe's young assistants spent time soaking up the sun and swimming in the waters surrounding the tropical island. They explored the many adjacent islands and old historic buildings of Bermuda that offered opportunities for sketching or water-color painting. When not on photo duty, Jack was frequently working on or around the boats which he loved, usually wearing a white yacht cap which quickly earned him the nickname Captain Jack. And always entertaining the whole crew was Beebe's pet capuchin monkey, named Chiriqui or Chiri for short, that he had acquired in 1925 when his expedition visited Panama as part of the exploration of the Galapagos. He was a loveable pet but could be mischievous at times, causing havoc among Beebe's toiletries by removing lids and making a mess, or getting into the laboratory and spilling chemicals and smashing test tubes.

5.5: Top: Beebe's birthday party on July 29 had a pirate theme. He stands at the back carrying a skull and crossbones sign, clasping a dagger between his teeth. Bottom (L to R): Llewellyn Miller water color painting; Jack as Captain Jack; Beebe with his pet monkey, Chiri.

With Beebe in Bermuda

Chapter 6

Arrival of the Bathysphere

The objective of the expedition shifted perceptibly when on May 10, 1930, Otis Barton arrived with the bathysphere. In advance of the arrival, an old barge named the *Ready* had been fitted out with steam winches and a derrick and boom designed to lift the two-and-a-half-ton sphere and retrieve it and its cabling from the depths. On a bathysphere dive day, the *Gladisfen* would leave the harbor area towing the *Ready* with the bathysphere on board, pick up the dive crew from Nonsuch and then sail out to the deep-dive area. Beebe and Tee-Van reckoned that from start to finish a dive would need a staff of around fifteen people, and it was imperative that everyone knew what job they were to do, so a number of test dives were planned.

On May 27, Beebe, Tee-Van and Jack Connery conducted the first bathysphere test dive in St. George's harbor to a depth of forty-five feet, checking for any leaks and assessing the oxygen system and the logistics for handling the sphere. Everything functioned perfectly and so the wait was on for a day of calm sea.

In the camp on the morning of June 6, after a quick breakfast, Beebe asked Tee-Van to go and tell Jack that he would be on the dive crew that day and his cameras needed to be working; then the two of them went aboard the *Skink* to prepare it to take the rest of the dive party out to the *Gladisfen*. Barton was already on the tugboat, having decided that camp life was not his thing, and preferring the home comforts of the St. George Hotel. There was a brief meeting between Beebe and Barton, then at the dive point out at sea, the tug stopped and there was a transfer of personnel to the *Ready*. Arthur Hollis and Jack went aft of the *Ready* to examine the winches, making sure there were no twists, and checked the gas tanks and connections on the Kohler generator. They had decided on an unmanned test dive to two thousand feet, after which, if all was well and the sea still calm, they would attempt a manned dive.

When they were ready, Tee-Van gave the signal to engage the boom winch and the bathysphere was lifted into the air, swung over the side and lowered into the ocean. After an hour at the deepest point, the sphere was brought back to the surface, dry and with no obvious problems. Jack was at hand to capture a number of photographs of the various stages of the unmanned test dive.

It was not yet mid-day, the sea was still calm and the bathysphere had just come back intact from a deeper descent than they were about to try. There was nothing left to do or say, but the next event needed to be recorded for posterity. Flags of the Explorers Club and the New York Zoological Society were fixed to the bathysphere, and Jack took a picture of Otis Barton and William Beebe together with the bathysphere to their left. The resultant print shows Beebe looking relaxed though perhaps a little distracted, and Barton looking worried and staring at the camera. Both men were aware of the high stakes involved and they were right to be worried: if the bathysphere fractured, or leaked in any major way, they would die not by drowning but by being pierced by high-speed water jets or immediately crushed by water pressure; if the winch failed and they could not be brought back to the surface their oxygen would only last a few hours; and if the cable holding the bathysphere broke, there would be no chance of a rescue.

6.1: Top: The bathysphere on the Ready being towed out to the deep dive area by the tugboat Gladisfen. Middle & Bottom: The bathysphere being being lifted in the air and lowered into the ocean for an unmanned test dive.

6.2: Jack Connery's iconic photograph of Barton and Beebe standing beside the flag-draped bathysphere in preparation for their record-breaking deep-sea dive on June 6, 1930.

Beebe and Barton laboriously clambered into the bathysphere through the fourteen-inch-diameter hatch and the door was screwed and pounded shut. Launch procedures were repeated and the sphere swung into the air, but a slight ocean swell caused it to swing like a pendulum and Beebe, concerned they may crash into the side of the *Ready*, fired a series of expletives through the telephone to the delicate ears of Gloria Hollister. Thankfully there was no collision and the bathysphere entered the ocean and started downwards.

In a later communication, Beebe recalled his impressions at the start of the descent. "The boundary of air and water above me appeared perfectly solid, and like a slowly waving, pale green canopy, quilted everywhere with deep, pale puckers – the sharp apexes of the wavelets above showing as smooth, rounded indentations below. The sunlight sifted down in long, oblique rays as if through some unearthly beautiful cathedral window." Always the master of the simile, metaphor or analogy, these descriptors by Beebe were a key feature of his prose and one of the reasons the books on his adventures had such universal appeal.

As they descended deeper, red was the first wavelength of light to disappear, and at fifty feet the dark-red shrimps on a book illustration that Beebe had brought with him appeared jet black. He and Barton were witnessing the gradual disappearance of each color in the rainbow as they were absorbed by the water above. At 400 feet, orange and yellow had vanished and green was greatly diminished. The record human aquatic descent at the time was a mere 525 feet, so at 600 feet, Beebe dramatically announced to Barton "only dead men have sunk below this." The ocean around them grew darker as they continued on down, and at 800 feet, Beebe called a halt to the dive. They were surrounded by the deepest blackest-blue imaginable and Beebe's intuition told him not to proceed any deeper. After five minutes at that depth, he gave the order to ascend and return to the surface. That day Beebe and Barton reached 803 feet – a new world record.

A few days later, on June 11, they descended to 1,426 feet, a little over a quarter of a mile and nearly three times deeper than any previous diver. This time they were a little more relaxed and Beebe was able to concentrate on the marine life visible through the porthole window of the bathysphere and report what he saw to Gloria Hollister. On the way down, he recognized many of the creatures from the net trawls, some with their own distinctive bioluminescence. Beebe described the inky blackness, broken only by the seemingly spontaneous light bursts emitted by many of the creatures, as a region akin to "naked space itself, out far beyond atmosphere, between the stars." At one point, he peered out and caught sight of an unfamiliar fish, about twenty feet long, that he described as "illuminated by myriads of tiny lights glittering like a diamond tiara." But even Beebe soon ran out of adequate words to describe an environment no one had ever seen before, falling back on the word brilliance to describe the total blackness. He commented later, "When once it has been seen, (the deep ocean) will remain the most vivid memory in life."

Current oceanographical opinion about marine life in deeper waters was that the absence of light and food together with the crushing pressures would mean there was little life and few large fish. Beebe and Barton's dive changed that view – the deep ocean was teeming with life and Beebe saw many fish, large and small, and far more than the random net trawling had suggested. And when the bathysphere was stationary, he had noted the presence of clouds of small particles continuously floating down through the water that he likened to 'marine snow'. It was the first direct observation of what is now recognized as an important food source for seafloor life. Returning to the surface was uneventful, and Jack was there to document the usual circus acrobatics Beebe and Barton had to perform in order to exit the vessel through the narrow hatch of the bathysphere.

6.3: *With the record broken, Beebe squeezes out through the fourteen-inch diameter hatch.*

Bad weather in the form of tropical storms and bad luck from several mechanical failures meant no more bathysphere dives that season. Jack had a bit of bad luck, too. In late summer, he slipped between the *Skink* and the wharf, injuring his back and had to retire from heavy lifting activities. The treatment was light work and rest, so he stayed on, helping where he could and developing and printing all his photographs. On days the sphere didn't descend, the team studied, drew and photographed dredged fish in the lab. Hollister often used her own system of chemical baths, dyes, and ultraviolet light, to decolor fish organs until they became translucent, revealing the red-stained skeleton and tail structures more clearly.

6.4: *Gloria Hollister developed various chemicals to decolored fish organs revealing the red-stained skeleton structure more clearly. This example shows Diplodus argenteus, a small inshore fish that inhabits reefs and coral and is known locally as the 'Bream of Bermuda'.*

In mid-July, Margaret Elliott and Llewellyn Miller returned to New York; in September, Perkins Bass, John Cannon and Jackson Guernsey did the same. The remaining members; the Beebes, Tee-Vann, Crouch, Zeigler, Barnes, Connery, Crane, and the Bostelmanns, Else and daughter Gertrude, returned to New York on the SS *Bermuda*, arriving back in New York on October 30, 1930, with 68 cases of specimens, books and instruments. Absent from the return trip was Jackson Patten, one of Beebe's young field assistants, who had been taken ill suddenly with acute appendicitis and despite the best efforts of doctors at the hospital had died on October 2. Beebe felt especial grief, partly blaming himself for the death of one of his most promising protégés and a potential future naturalist.

Over the winter of 1930, Beebe wrote of his experiences in an article for the National Geographic magazine, published in June 1931, entitled *A Round Trip to Davy Jones' Locker*. It featured thirteen of Jack's photographs of the bathysphere being launched and retrieved, including the one with Beebe and Barton posing alongside it. The article resulted in much publicity for Beebe and helped secure financial sponsorship of the bathysphere from the society on future expeditions. Beebe and Barton were to return to Bermuda again in 1932 and 1934 to achieve a dive of a half-mile, but the photographs taken by Jack Connery in 1930 were widely circulated and have become the defining images of the record-breaking Beebe/Barton deep-sea dives in the bathysphere.

Chapter 7

Return to Florida & Rollins College

After more than six months of excitement, exploring, observing, and photographing marine life with one of the nation's top naturalists, Jack unsurprisingly felt a sense of anticlimax as he returned to Orlando at the beginning of November 1930. He picked up his ornithology work again with Carl Dann and Joe Howell and went on a few eagles' nest and egg collecting outings and wondered what to do with the rest of his life. He wanted to share his experiences of the natural world, particularly with younger people, and realized that he had stories to tell relating both to ornithology and to marine science. He started with the topic of his time in Bermuda, embarking on a series of school, scout and society talks in the Orlando area, and in support the local newspaper published details of the expedition and included his wonderment as he explored the seabed in a diving helmet and experienced its huge variety of colorful lifeforms.

As a member of the Florida Audubon Society, he was also frequently in demand to give presentations on bird life at local society meetings, or to organize school trips to bird sanctuaries. His colleague, golfer Carl Dann, gave presentations too, but always seemed to attract larger audiences at talks about birds with his ability to make sure the words 'birdies' and 'eagles' appeared in the title and throughout his talks. When speaking to young audiences at school events, Jack would use his own projector and screen and show slides of his photographs of many of Florida's most interesting and little-known birds, emphasizing how patience was needed in order to get the perfect photograph. He stressed how wrong it was to kill birds, and got the youngsters to repeat the rhyme "Shooting birds is vicious sport with a gun; shoot them with a camera, it is much more fun!"

He recalled an article he'd written back in 1928 for the local paper stressing the way that nature defines every aspect of existence but remains hidden to most people. He argued that the typical businessman uses paper and pencil without thinking that they are products of the natural world, and the average person knows few flowers or plants, nor can identify them. He stated that it would be safe to say that most people do not know what the birds are here for. He finished with the contention that nature is fundamental in every undertaking and every accomplishment, and suggested that although we can't all be experts, at least we can strive to know a little of nature's workings.

Jack was a hands-on naturalist having seen firsthand the wonder and teeming variety of the undersea world with William Beebe, experienced the intimacy of an egret rookery with Oscar Baynard, and examined closeup the intricate beauty of the flowers of Theodore Mead's prize orchids. Although not particularly academically inclined, he noted that Carl Dann was already a sophomore at Rollins College in Winter Park, Joe Howell was shortly expected to go and study there, and all the young field assistants he had interacted with on the Beebe expedition were college-educated to some extent. He concluded that he needed to go back to school to be taken more seriously as a naturalist.

Although he had no money, Connery approached Rollins College with a view to studying there, and reached an agreement that he would donate his extensive collection of bird's eggs and nests to the Thomas R. Baker Museum of Natural History at the College in exchange for tuition. The museum already contained numerous examples of artifacts in ornithology, entomology, zoology and geology and occupied a floor in Knowles Hall, but was currently without leadership following the death in May 1930 of its founder Dr. Baker. The arrangement was that Jack would become student curator of the museum, tasked with organizing and expanding the museum's collections, and would be required to assist with the teaching of some botany and ornithology lessons, but in return could sit in on all these and associated classes.

7.1: *Theodore Mead outside his house* Wait-a-bit *in Oviedo with one of his prize orchids, January 1932. His entire orchid collection of hundreds of plants was on display when the Mead Botanical Garden opened in 1940.*

As part of enrolling at Rollins College, Jack got to know Dr. Edwin Grover, Professor of Books, and learned of their shared friendship and admiration for horticulturist Theodore Mead of Oviedo. On returning to Orlando, Jack had renewed his acquaintance with his old scouting associate and throughout the early 1930s was a frequent visitor to see Mead at his gardens by the shore of Lake Charm. As part of his Rollins teaching commitments in botany, Jack also started to take parties of Rollins' students to Mead's estate and greenhouse and see firsthand the process of plant hybridization.

Aware of Mead's increasing fragility, Jack became his willing assistant, helping with tasks such as repotting orchids in the greenhouse, digging and dividing amaryllis bulbs, or collecting and planting caladium seeds. He started to document the orchid collection and borrowed Mead's orchid negatives to make into colored lantern slides for presentation purposes. On one occasion as they rested after their horticultural labors, he said, "Someday I am going to build a memorial garden for you." Mead had modestly waved the suggestion aside, but Jack meant it.

7.2: Left: On July 4, 1932, the Connerys took Theodore Mead for an outing to Daytona Beach; the image shows Mead with two of the younger Connery siblings. Right: Mead sits on a rustic bench by the pool in the garden of 741 W. Colonial Drive on his eighty-first birthday, February 23, 1933.

Recognizing Mead's declining mobility, Jack drove him to various events and meetings, entertained him to dinner at the Connery house, and took him on seaside outings. Through his camera work, he continued to record aspects of Mead's life, and on Independence Day, 1932, the Connerys took Mead for a day out to Daytona Beach. Theo's diary recorded the event; "I had a fine time Sunday, July 3 – my scout friend Jack Connery, who is instructor in birds and plants at Rollins College, came over to invite me to dinner at his home in Orlando and then next day made up a party for Daytona Beach. Camped on the ocean beach – good grub and fine time and got back about 9 p.m. I expected to drive my car home but the folks knew I hated to drive at night so Jack drove my car for me and Mr. & Mrs. Connery tagged along in another car to take Jack home. Awfully nice of them because I really do hate to drive at night all alone."

Theodore Mead dined with the Connerys on many occasions, but February 23, 1933 was a special one, his eighty-first birthday, warranting a surprise party at their Orlando home. There were fifteen guests, a huge cake with candles on it, and a place-card at every seat with a medallion photograph of Mead on it, which he was asked to autograph. Before they ate, he walked the Connery garden and sat on the rustic bench beside the garden pond for Jack to take his photograph.

Although still looking for a new adventure, Jack's life would change in quite a different way than he expected when he fell head-over-heels in love with a Rollins student who had started at the same time as him. Helen Golloway followed in her elder sister's footsteps in coming to Rollins from their home in North Canton, Ohio. Her sister K. Iverne Golloway (also written Galloway) was a 1929 senior at Rollins, active in her time in college life and a budding fictional book author, initially of detective fiction but later as a writer of children's stories under the pseudonym of Elizabeth Ireland. Jack met Helen towards the end of 1931 and by the middle of the next year they had become engaged.

The pair were inseparable and he took her to Oviedo and introduced Theodore Mead to her as 'Uncle Teddy', who showed her round his house. Helen recalled her first impressions of the interior living rooms, "On the mantle Mr. Mead has a clock which shows the date and the phases of the moon and season, as well as the hour. In his study is a very rare collection of stamps and postcards, copies of the Bible in many languages, a microscope, chairs from his grandmother's wedding set, and all kinds of classics and scientific books; on a table rest several albums containing hand-tinted photographs he has made of his orchids."

7.3: Jack Connery and Helen Golloway, circa 1933.

Following their engagement, the two families got to know each other and the Golloways came down to enjoy the Florida sights, including a trip to the gardens at Bok Tower. Helen went on outings to the beach to get to know the rest of the Connery clan, and both she and Jack joined in college life by enrolling in the internationally-focused Cosmopolitan Club.

7.4: The Connery family at Daytona Beach, circa 1933. From L to R: Bill, Charlie, Tom, Tom's wife Grace, Thelma, Thelma's boyfriend Marion Harvey, Helen Golloway, and Jack.

Return to Florida & Rollins College

When Jack took over stewardship of the Baker Museum in 1931, he recognized he could do with help in cataloging and collating the collections. The logical mind and well-organized skills of Helen met this need and he arranged for her to work with him at the museum as secretary and assistant. He also sought advice from the naturalist-inclined academic members of the college about their areas of expertise and interest, so the museum could better relate to subjects that they were teaching. A chance event in September 1931 presented a likely candidate when a student at the college, Miss Thelma Van Buskirk, brought to the museum a tusk and a tooth found by her brother, US Government official Mr. Allen Van Buskirk, during his inspection of canal dredging near Flagler Beach, Florida. The fossils were subsequently identified and determined by the Smithsonian Institute to be mastodon remains. Jack visited the site on the Bon Terra Estate eight miles north of Flagler Beach with Van Buskirk, who told him that a friend had recently struck some bones near-by while plowing.

Jack decided to create an informal Explorers Club at the college to explore local undeveloped areas, such as Flagler Beach, and conduct a scientific search for artifacts that could end up in the Baker museum's collections. As a natural leader, he quickly signed up like-minded students who were interested in joining these fossil-hunting outings.

The academic experts at Rollins identified a second potential site for fossils at nearby Kelly Park, near Apopka. Here it was believed that remains of extinct land mammals would be found in the rock formations about the country park, which was given to Orange County several years ago. With the sanction of President Hamilton Holt, a petition was presented to the Orange County commissioners by Dr. Charles Campbell, Professor of Entomology at Rollins College, Edwin Grover, and Jack Connery for permission to excavate in the park. The commissioners gave their tentative approval subject to the trees and foliage of the park being protected while the work was being conducted, but left the final decision to John Hopkins University who originally gave the park to the county.

In early February 1932, Ed Johnson, owner of the property at Bon Terra, granted permission for Rollins College to excavate, so exploration of the Kelly Park site was put to one side for the time being in favor of a location with known fossil remains. Jack assembled a party of five Explorers Club students and, with visiting faculty instructor Dr. Frank Armitage, headed out to Flagler Beach. They started to excavate about ten paces from where the plow struck bones and found several vertebrate fossils in the water-logged muck trench, before discovering a submerged large solid bone object. Jack reached his hand underneath and into a cavity from which he drew out a chert arrowhead with a broken point. Several bone needle parts were found nearby and the close association between these man-made objects and the bones had everyone excited. The large object proved to be a pair of mammoth's lower jaws with teeth which was successfully freed from the mud and brought to the surface with the assistance of students Bob Maclay, Doug Riggs, and Dan Havens, who then posed with the jaws for Jack to snap the photograph.

7.5: *Rollins College students Robert Maclay, Douglas Riggs, and Daniel Havens carry the excavated jawbones of a prehistoric mammoth from the digging area at Flagler Beach, Florida, in early February, 1932.*

Mammoth and mastodon fossils had been found elsewhere in North America, including around the coast of Florida, so this was a significant find in agreement with the widely held view that giant mammals had stalked the Florida peninsula in prehistoric times. But this was only the third site in Florida, after Vero (1916) and Melbourne (1922), where human remains or manmade artifacts were discovered in close association with the mammal remains, pointing to a possible co-existence of man and mammoth. This possibility had previously been dismissed by mainstream archaeological experts who almost universally believed at that time that humans were not in Florida early enough to interact with mammoths.

Government scientists visited the site, examined the artifacts, and warned against jumping to conclusions. How could a young enthusiastic college student with no formal archaeological training discover something that might overturn the established view of when the first Americans arrived in Florida? Jack was active writing up the findings and, with the help of Rollins' academics, created a teaser piece for the May 1932 issue of *Science* journal. Aware of possible controversy, his cautious conclusions read "Excavations are being continued in the hope of obtaining additional data which may possibly prove of value in connection with the question as to the antiquity of man on this continent."

Newspapers got hold of this story and had no problem making the man-mammoth association, with headlines such as: "Arrowhead Found in Skull Shows Man and Mammoth Lived Together in Florida." The result was major publicity for Rollins College, the Baker Museum, and Jack's reputation as a naturalist. Despite the publicity, the college was in the throes of the Great Depression at that time and there was no funding available for further excavation, even though at the site parts of several other large boney structures could be seen buried in the mud.

One of Jack's closest Explorers Club friends was Carrington Lloyd, a science student from Massachusetts. Despite lack of financial support, he and Jack kept the fossil hunting flame alive, and in October 1932 they made a series of expeditions down the St. Johns River excavating Indian mounds, discovering three Indian skulls and collections of various bones. With the end of the year approaching, there was some good news as far as funding was concerned. On December 14, 1932, Jack Connery announced that an anonymous donor had given Rollins College a gift of $1,000 to continue the excavations at Flagler Beach. The donor turned out to be Carrington Lloyd's mother, and A. J. Hanna of the College wrote a note to Hamilton Holt explaining the background to the gift. "Mrs. Henry D. Lloyd has just sent $1,000 to be used for Jack Connery and his digging. Jack is just recuperating from an appendicitis operation and I guess they had a hard time keeping him in bed when he heard of all that money. Mrs. Lloyd's son, Carrington, it seems is very intimate with Jack and I suppose it was thru his interest in Jack's work that she gave the money."

Over the Christmas holidays of 1932, Jack and his colleagues started excavating again at the Flagler Beach site, hoping to unearth the partially buried bones which they thought might turn out to be an entire mammoth skeleton. The large bones proved to be in very poor condition and a decision was made not to remove them, but smaller bones were brought back to Rollins for microscopic examination. Overall, despite excavating an area of around twenty-square feet, the results were disappointing compared to the finds of the first dig.

Still keen to acquire fossils for the museum, and with money from the Lloyds left in the pot, Jack organized an Explorers Club trip in January 1933 to the area of Homosassa Springs. Their intention was to look around the old Yulee Sugar Mill, then go to the Sabertooth Cave where a complete upper canine of the sabertooth cat was discovered in 1928, and finally visit Clarks Quarry, an abandoned stone excavation where they hoped to find more fossil remains. The party consisted of Jack and Helen, students Bill Crider, Carrington Lloyd, Jack Fischer, Eileen Christianson, Douglas Riggs, Helen Welch, and Dave Bothe, with Edwin Grover and J. E. Spurr, Professor of Geology, representing the staff of Rollins College. They spent the morning at the sugar mill where they were surprised to see much of the original machinery intact, before lunching at a hotel in Homosassa. The Sabertooth Cave proved to be a massive cavern 175 feet long, 57 feet in width and four feet high, only reached by a ladder down through a small hole in the ground. Inside the cavern, high up, was another narrow passage which once reached and entered revealed a chamber filled with stalagmites and stalactites of all shapes and sizes. A few pristine specimens were carefully removed for the museum collection, then on to Clarks Quarry, where they picked up many beautiful crystalline specimens and found part of a fossil rib-bone and a fossil sea conch as big as an ostrich egg. With the sun setting, they returned to Winter Park where Dave Bothe wrote up the day's adventure for the college *Sandspur* newspaper.

7.6: Jack Connery at Highlands Hammock, near Sebring, Florida, in March 1933 excavating a 35,000-year-old giant turtle fossil. Photograph by Helen Golloway.

Jack's publicity from the Flagler Beach fossil dig led to him being contacted by authorities at Highlands Hammock, near Sebring, where fragments of bone had been found as workmen were laying a pipeline through an orange grove near the hammock entrance. Jack, Helen and several members of the Explorers Club went down to Sebring and started digging, shoring up the ditch with supports as they went. They came across a large fossil object almost completely buried but with a complete elephant tusk above it, which they extracted and laid on the ditch bank. As they were preparing to coat the tusk with shellac to protect it from degradation, it disintegrated with an almost imperceptible hissing sound.

Jack then turned his attention to the large object which looked like the upturned fossilized remains of an animal. He and Helen carefully scraped the soil off a few square inches at a time and then applied a coating of shellac to exclude the air. After hours of patient work the fossil was fully uncovered and brought to the surface with a wooden tripod hoist fitted with a block and tackle. Experts identified the remains as that of a giant prehistoric turtle which when alive more than 35,000 years ago would have measured nearly three feet high, four feet across and five feet long and would have weighed about a ton. They concluded that it was a near relative of the Testudo family of land turtles, similar to the giant turtles found on the Galapagos Islands. Today the fossil can be seen inside the exploration center at Hammock Inn by the entrance to Highlands Hammock State Park.

7.7: The turtle fossil today on display at Highlands Hammock State Park.

During the time Jack and Helen were excavating the turtle fossil in March 1933, Highlands Hammock were running a series of early Florida historical pageant days that included several Seminole Indians and their families camping in the hammock. Among the Seminoles were Charlie Cypress, an Everglades guide, and his family; Lea Cypress, daughter of the late medicine man Conapatchee and a descendent of the famous Chief Osceola; Richard Osceola; George Osceola;

and Frank Cypress and Charlie Fewell and their families. One of the four pageants featured the acting and telling of Indian legends set inside a village constructed of open-air, thatched-roof houses known as chickees. Jack used his camera to capture some of the activities of these proud people who were part of Florida's original native population, including one showing their curiosity over the workings of the Highlands Hammock Austin American panel van.

7.8: *During the time Jack was excavating the turtle fossil, there was a Seminole Indian pageant at the site. Here a group inspect the engine and workings of the Highlands Hammock Austin American panel van.*

In late 1933, Jack and Helen's time at Rollins College came to an end and they set about planning their marriage for the following year and their future together. This also marked the end of the Explorers Club as envisaged by Jack – a group of enthusiastic students whose interests were in exploring the history of Florida and its undeveloped regions and finding educational artifacts for the Baker Museum. The museum was now leaderless again until September 1934, when President Holt appointed Edward M. Davis as Director. In 1939, plans were hatched to move the museum off campus to the Aloma Country Club, but this appears to have failed presumably because of lack of funding. The fate of the extensive natural history collections, including the Flagler Beach mammoth jaw, is undocumented but they were probably donated to various other museums in Central Florida.

The Flagler Beach findings had brought publicity and credit to Rollins College and were subject to a reevaluation in 1953 by Floridian archaeologist Wilfred T. Neill. He visited the Bon Terra site but found there was nothing left to see; by this time the site owners had cannibalized the diggings for artifacts they could sell to tourists at local novelty shops. But he examined Connery's arrowhead, which Connery had taken away for safekeeping, and decided that it was in fact a stemmed scraper, a type of artifact known to be much later than when the bones would have been deposited. His conclusion was that the association between artifacts and extinct vertebrates was purely a fortuitous one.

This analysis was the unfortunate result of the archaeological default position at the time: that the continent of North America was initially populated solely by large-game hunters who crossed the Bering Straits land bridge approximately 12,000 years ago, and upon their arrival promptly hunted mammoths to extinction. This belief persisted for the next forty years as the Clovis-first theory, until renown University of Florida archaeologist and anthropologist Charles A. Hoffman began an excavation in 1973 that produced compelling evidence for prehistoric man and animals having lived together in Florida before the land bridge was established. Even then some refused to be convinced by the evidence that suggested that the earliest population of the continent consisted of several groups of people that used various land and seafaring access routes and arrived at different times, some earlier than 12,000 years ago. Nowadays most scientists reject the idea that the first Americans came by land and the Clovis-first theory has been comprehensively debunked.

7.9: The chert arrowhead with the broken tip that Jack Connery found embedded in a cavity of the prehistoric mammoth jawbone excavated at Flagler Beach. The find suggested that man and mammoth coexisted at the same time in early Florida history, an idea that was soundly rejected by archaeological experts of the period but has widespread acceptance today.

In 2000, Hoffman, by then a retired professor of anthropology at Northern Arizona University, started work on a review article on early man in Florida and came across Connery's work and the paper he'd written in 1932. He wrote to Rollins College asking whether Jack was still alive and whether the artifacts he discovered were still at the Baker Museum, as he would like to photograph them. He attached a short extract from the review paper, where he described the Flagler Beach excavation of 1932 as 'most intriguing' and Jack's report of the work as 'truly amazing'. This was a vindication of Jack Connery's excavation of the mammoth and the discovery of the arrowhead at Flagler Beach. It helped bring about a reconsideration of who the first American colonizers were and how and when they arrived, although unfortunately Jack wasn't around to appreciate his small contribution to putting an early nail in the coffin of the Clovis-first theory, having died in 1982.

Chapter 8

Marriage & Mead Botanical Garden

Jack Connery and Helen Golloway were married on May 30, 1934 in North Canton, Ohio, in the study of the North Canton Community Christian church, just a few blocks away from her home at 610 N. Main Street. It was a very quiet affair with Mr. and Mrs. Golloway the only guests, Reverend M. A. Cossaboom officiating, and Helen looking very demure, dressed in white and carrying a bouquet of red rose buds.

Immediately after the ceremony, they left for a short honeymoon at Lookout Mountain, an area that Jack knew well from his Chattanooga childhood days. Just six miles from downtown Chattanooga, the area was one that Jack kept coming back to, a place of soaring rock formations, caves, and lush gardens. As a boy, and in the company of his elder brothers, he loved riding the incline railway to the top and gazing at the magnificent panoramic view of Moccasin Bend in the Tennessee River, with the bird's eye view of the city of Chattanooga in the distance. He would squeeze through the stone passages of Rock City, explore the meandering trails to the summit, and wonder at the ancient rock formations and caverns. Usually carrying a camera or pair of binoculars, these experiences at Lookout Mountain were most likely the ones that had given him his first taste of the beauty, diversity, and grandeur of the natural world.

8.1: Jack Connery married Helen Golloway, a fellow student at Rollins College, on May 30, 1934, in North Canton, Ohio. Jack and Helen became essential figures in the early development and running of Mead Botanical Garden.

After the short honeymoon, Jack and Helen returned to live with Helen's parents in North Canton. Jack's father-in-law, like most people in the town, worked at the giant Hoover Vacuum Cleaner Company factory as a machine shop supervisor and was able to find Jack a job there as an inspector. But Ohio was not Florida and before the end of 1934 they had returned to Orlando, where most of Jack's family and people he knew were, renting property at 710 N. Westmoreland Drive, a couple of blocks from his parent's home. He also had relatives in the area – the Brogdens – who were close social friends of the family and related to Jack via the marriage of his mother's sister, an Englerth, to Mr. Ernest Brogden. In September 1935, the Brogden's daughter, Eleanor, married Paul Carr Palmer in the garden overlooking the lake at 741 W. Colonial Drive, with Jack acting as groomsman.

8.2: Lookout Mountain near Chattanooga was one of Jack's favorite places that he knew and explored as a boy, riding the incline to the top with his older brothers (top left). He spent his honeymoon there in 1934 with Helen (top right), and returned often in his younger years to gaze at the panoramic view of Chattanooga from Lookout Point (bottom left), or squeeze through the narrow passages at Rock City (bottom right).

Ernest Brogden had established two small companies in Orlando; Mutual Fruit Distributors Inc., and the Fruit Treating Corporation, both involved in the cleaning and coating of citrus and other fruits and vegetables and the use of food-grade dyes for coloring citrus juice. The principal product was a borax-based solution used for coating fruit to extend shelf life by preventing early fungal infection by molds, based on a patent granted in 1933. It had particular application to citrus fruit which when stored often developed a blue mold in the crannies of the skin, leading to rapid fungal decay and resulting in significant losses for fruit growers and packers. Brogden offered his nephew a job, initially as a salesman and then as assistant chemist in their laboratories, researching other applications of the borax treatment.

Shortly after their return to Orlando, Helen became pregnant and subsequently gave birth to a boy, John H. Jr., on October 5, 1935. The Connery family were never one to call their children simply by their birth certificate name, so, like his father, he became universally known as Jack Jr. or simply Jackie.

Although busy with their family, Jack and Helen tried to see Theodore Mead at Oviedo as often as they could. Jack had told Helen of his dream of making a memorial garden for Theodore Mead and with Mead's approval, she started getting copies of his diaries, letters and information about the parentage of Mead's various orchid hybridizations. At this point in late 1935, Mead was increasingly unsteady, hard of hearing and had given up driving to his loyal chauffeur/handyman, Clayton Newton. He was being looked after by Libbie Wainright, a devoted and caring lady whom he had known for years and whose son Bennie had been one of Mead's scouts in the 1920s. She lived a short walk away on Lake Charm Circle.

The inevitable happened on April 24, 1936, when Mead suffered a massive stroke at his *Wait-a-Bit* home. Within 36 hours he was taken to the Fernald-Laughton Hospital in Sanford but by then the damage was irreversible, and he died peacefully in his sleep on May 4. Funeral services took place at St. Luke's Cathedral in Orlando at 4:30 p.m. on Wednesday, May 7, 1936, officiated by

Dean Melville Johnson. Jack took charge of organizing five ex-scouts from his Oviedo troop, Emmett Kelsey, Arthur Partin, J. E. Jones, Jr., Ewan Jones, and Allen Thompson, who together with him would bear the casket. The church was filled with a mass of floral tributes as befitting the great horticulturist, and interment took place at the family grave in Greenwood cemetery, Orlando, lot 119, section B, with the death certificate recording his age as 84 years, 2 months, and 11 days.

With the passing of Theodore Mead, Jack had inherited a number of problems, the first of which was a question concerning the ownership of Mead's plants. Mead had written his will in 1933 and clearly stated that all his greenhouse plants should be given to the Royal Palm State Park in the Everglades, then sponsored by the Federation of Women's Clubs. In 1916, he had made an early donation of some of his orchids to the park and they had been placed high in the trees by the plant house in an area referred to as the Mead Orchid Garden. Unfortunately, a severe Florida freeze in December 1934 had killed all of them and many other cold-sensitive plants at the park, resulting in Mead changing his mind but not the words in his will. Subsequently he had promised by letter that half of the orchids should go to Mr. Clifford Cole of Coral Gables, Miami and, verbally, the other half to Jack. Augustus Willis, the Coalburgh, West Virginia, executor of the will on behalf of Mead's two nieces, contacted the federation who passed a resolution relinquishing all claims and giving all the plants to him, who then looked to Cole and Connery to sort things out. Cole did not want to split the collection and, knowing of Jack's plans for a memorial garden, generously gave his share to Jack. Not all saw it that way however, and a Miami newspaper ran a story characterizing Cole's gesture as "Fortune in Blooming Treasure Given away by Miami Family."

With the orchid ownership solved, Jack turned his attention to the second problem – one of a suitable location. There were some who thought that the memorial garden ought to be in Oviedo at the Mead estate. As early as June 1936, the Orange County and Greater Orlando Chamber of Commerce beautification committee had proposed that the tract be designated a State Park. Their members visited the estate to gather data on which to base an appeal for state assistance but the application did not succeed. A little later, Willis received an audacious letter from Edwin Grover asking whether he would consider gifting the Oviedo estate in its entirety to Rollins College. He suggested it could be known as the "Mead Arboretum and Botanical Garden," and his brother Frederick, recently retired as Professor of Botany at Oberlin College, might be persuaded to become its director and develop its use as a teaching and research aid for science students from Rollins. Meanwhile Jack was talking to officials in the park department of the city of Orlando, who were keen on the idea of an Orlando botanical garden, and had suggested a location at the east end of Lake Eola, down by the old concrete tennis courts.

Finally, there was the concern about looking after the welfare of the plants, possibly through two or three cold winters, until he had an agreed location. There was also the worry about plant theft. Libbie Wainright was kept on as caretaker at Oviedo, but she was not fulltime and the estate was frequently wide-open to opportunists who might steal some of the rarer plants, either from the greenhouse or from the barn where many of the bulbous plants were stored for the winter.

Jack and Helen moved to a larger rented property at 2346 Fairbanks Avenue in Winter Park to give them space to start collecting and protecting Mead's plants. Jack already had over 20,000 Mead-strain amaryllis bulbs which Mead had said he could have before he died, and these were laid out to dry on the floor of the garage. Jack planted various azaleas and small palms from Oviedo in the garden and filled the small greenhouse there with as many orchids as he could. Willis had finally agreed that in addition to all the orchids Jack could take any easily-moveable plants from the estate for the memorial garden, so long as it still looked presentable to a potential purchaser.

Jack and Helen were out in Winter Park one Sunday afternoon and called in to see Edwin Grover at his house. Talk turned to a memorial garden for Mead, and Grover told him that Rollins wanted to acquire the Oviedo estate as a botanical garden for Rollins' students. Jack said he had a better idea and described a tract of land in the south of Winter Park, bordering on Orlando, that had a stream running through it, a small lake, and a rookery. He also knew who owned it – Orlando real estate developer Walter Rose. It needed investigating so next morning, accompanied by Robert Mitchell a qualified landscaping architect, Jack and Edwin Grover set out with high boots on and hatchets in hand. They cut their way through the underbrush until they found the lake across from which was a rookery filled with nesting herons and egrets. As they made their way along the shore, they were greeted with an eruption of noise and feathers as hundreds of birds took to the air. Once they had settled back down, Jack sat on Grover's shoulders and took several photographs of a nest with heron's eggs in it and several of the snowy egrets, with one of the photographs Grover later describing as 'a beautiful one'. They explored the swamp, the stream and the wooded areas, and decided this was indeed the place for a botanical garden.

8.3: *Jack Connery's 1937 photograph of rookery residents at the lake in the future site of Mead Botanical Garden, taken by Jack sitting on Edwin Grover's shoulders.*

The city of Winter Park got right behind the idea, and in April 1937 Mayor Moody appointed a committee to apply for a Works Progress Administration (WPA) grant for the development of the proposed garden. While the paperwork was going through the system, Jack had plenty of free time to plan how the garden might look and what features it might have. First and foremost, he wanted to honor the man who had revealed the world of plants to him – his botanical mentor and friend Theodore Mead. But it was big ideas time and Jack suggested the possibility of including an aviary and even a sea aquarium. They turned to Robert Mitchell, the Florida horticulturist and landscape architect who had explored the jungle swamp with them, to make a detailed plan of the garden. He had studied horticulture in St. Louis at the Missouri Botanical Garden, returning to Florida in 1929 to manage James Hendry's Everglades Nursery, then starting up his own Shore Acres foliage nursery in Kissimmee in 1930. Mitchell's plan incorporated all of Jack's three areas; a large greenhouse complex by the Orlando entrance, a spacious aviary spanning Howell Creek, and a purpose-built salt-water aquarium with direct access from S. Pennsylvania Avenue in Winter Park.

Many thought Jack's ideas were fanciful and unworkable, particularly the sea aquarium which some people had problems with understanding how salt water fish could be kept alive in an inland aquarium. But Jack had thought this through and pointed to the fact that the Chicago aquarium obtained its salt water from Miami, delivered via tank cars. The water was filtered at regular intervals and used for more than a year before needing replacement.

In anticipation of the garden being given the go-ahead, Jack started constructing a wooden greenhouse with a part-glass roof on the Leedy-donated plot by the Winter Park entrance on S. Pennsylvania Avenue. Jack, Helen and young Jackie moved close-by into a new rental property on the avenue at number 1099 to keep an eye on the greenhouse and its bulging contents of valuable orchids. Jack still fussed about the possibility of break-ins and even went as far as on one occasion to hire armed guards to protect the contents of the greenhouse when he had to go away for a short time.

8.4: Before Mead Botanical Garden opened, Jack Connery built a temporary wooden greenhouse with a part-glass roof close to the Winter Park entrance to house many of Mead's prize orchids.

By December 1937, the news from Washington was that the initial grant for $20,170 had been approved and that they were willing to supplement this fund as the work progressed. They did, however, require the City of Winter Park to contribute matching funds at this stage. The city was in poor financial shape due to the depression and was incapable of meeting this requirement, but Jack Connery came to the rescue – agreeing to bequeath all of Mead's plants in lieu of cash. With several thousand caladium and amaryllis bulbs, several hundred azalea plants and more than one thousand orchids, many of which were unusual hybrids worth hundreds of dollars each, the total value of the plants donated easily met this figure.

The first spade of earth to start the development of the garden was turned by Florida Senator Charles Andrews at an official groundbreaking ceremony on January 8, 1938. Dignitaries were present and speeches given, which included one by Grover who confirmed Jack's position as director and Helen's as secretary of the garden. He recognized Jack's contribution and vision in creating the botanical garden by stating, "For nine years Jack cherished this dream. Today this dream is a reality."

The WPA work force started on January 17, initially deepening Howell Creek by three feet to help drain the adjoining swamp area so that trails could be laid, and preparing the drained land ready for the planting of azaleas and other shrubs that required rich peat soil. Other major initial tasks were the erection of nearly two miles of fencing supported by cabbage palm posts, the clearing of the entire property of underbrush, and the creation of a number of mirror pools along Howell Creek. One day, soon after the first few trails had been cleared and laid with clay and sawdust, Martin Andersen, proprietor of the Orlando newspaper, came walking along and met Jack and Edwin Grover at the Winter Park gate. Grover later recalled Andersen's comments following what he had just experienced as, "This is the finest thing that has happened to Central Florida. Who is, or did he say who the devil is, responsible for it?" From that moment on, Andersen's help and generosity towards the garden was secured.

As director of the garden, Jack was in charge of the work that the WPA labor force performed, while paid WPA supervisors took care of their pay and hours worked. Since the start the average contingent of workers was around fifty per day, so the workload required planning and organizing. Jack was a born leader and a hands-on boss who never asked anyone to do a job that he couldn't do himself. He was immensely popular with all the workmen, with his enthusiasm, personal warmth and friendliness, and universally known as Jack. He had a productive relationship with Edwin Grover which initially was based on mutual respect but slowly led to a lasting friendship. Grover's son Graham, a disturbed young man, joined the workforce and Jack spent much time guiding and helping him with various horticultural tasks. Jack and Helen's second son had been born in October 1937 and had been named Edwin in honor of Grover. When it came time for his baptism in May 1938 at Knowles Memorial Chapel at Rollins College, Grover was honored to be godfather in a ceremony conducted by Dean Charles A. Campbell with the assistance of President Hamilton Holt.

8.5: *Edwin Grover, as godfather, holds baby Edwin Connery on the occasion of his baptism at Knowles Chapel, Rollins College on May 29, 1938. On the reverse of the photograph Helen lists the others as, L to R; Dean Campbell, Aunt Bess, Helen, Jackie held by Joe Connery, Viola Connery, and Hamilton Holt.*

Throughout the first part of 1939, more preparative work took place in the garden with the emphasis on clearing and grubbing areas of land ready for planting. Jack started hauling in hundreds of cabbage palms from Oviedo and planting them to create a tropical feel. From the Everglades he brought more palms in other varieties, including Royal, Washingtonia, Fishtail, Coconut, Cane, and Phoenix. He became an expert at digging up, transporting and transplanting palms. As

Grover recalled much later, "There wasn't a palm tree in the entire Garden; Jack put in every one that is there today. He was told he could take as many palms as he wanted from one location, and he transplanted nearly a thousand of them." As the year progressed, and with a target date of January 1940 set for opening, the pace of work accelerated and 250 gardenias and 2,000 azaleas and camellias were brought in and planted together with a run of 225 feet of sweet peas by the Orlando entrance. Masses of colorful annuals – salvias, calendulas, snapdragons, pansies, carnations, larkspur and many others – were planted in the hillside garden that sloped down to one of the mirror pools.

A supplementary WPA grant of $42,000 had been awarded in early 1939 to allow the work on the garden to be completed, but this just provided wages for the workers and could not be used for capital or running expenses. Both Jack and Edwin Grover had on occasions to put their hand in their pockets to pay for things like gas for the truck. By September 1939, they badly needed cash in order to complete the Garden and get it ready for opening. A key requirement was for a large greenhouse at the Orlando entrance to showcase the vast collection of rare and beautiful Mead orchids. Fate took a hand in filling this need. John Anthony Porter, the owner of one of the most beautiful gardens in Edgewater Heights, Orlando, had unfortunately recently passed away. A keen horticulturist with an impressive garden display of camellias and azaleas, he had just installed a $1,200 greenhouse but died before he had time to fill it with plants. Mrs. Porter was offering it to the Garden for $350, but the immediate problem was raising the money to buy it and have it professionally dismantled and reinstalled in the garden.

In late September 1939, Martin Andersen received a tour of the Garden and was amazed at the progress achieved. Connery and Grover poured their hearts out to him over the financial state they were in, with over $10,000 needed to meet the January opening date. Andersen committed to help them get the money and wasted no time moving into action. True to his word, the next day he wrote an editorial describing the Garden as 'an invaluable asset' and praising the efforts and personal sacrifices of Connery and Grover. He kept the campaign up to raise the money, encouraging, cajoling and occasionally berating Central Florida residents and business to give money to the fund. One such appeal ran, "Theodore Mead was called to another country from his labors to make this world a more beautiful place. The products of a life's work are now in degree being transferred to the Mead Botanical Garden. If Winter Park and Orlando really desire to have something unique, beautiful and educational, now's the opportunity."

8.6: The magnificent Porter greenhouse filled with orchids at the Orlando entrance to Mead Botanical Garden, circa 1940.

In a little over a week, the target had been reached, triggering a grateful Grover to write to Andersen, "Without your co-operation and that of your newspapers, the campaign could not have succeeded as it has." There is little doubt that without the personal urgings of Martin Andersen the opening of Mead Botanical Garden might never have happened.

8.7: *Top: Hamilton Holt and Edwin Grover lead a selection of the dignitaries on a stroll round Mead Botanical Garden on opening day, January 14, 1940. Middle: Senator Charles Andrews, Jack Connery, and Senator Claude Pepper and his wife admire the artist impression of the planned aquarium (closeup, bottom).*

Opening day on January 14, 1940, was a huge success with nearly three thousand people attending the official ceremonies, including both the Florida senators, Claude Pepper and Charles Andrews, their wives, and the mayors of Orlando and Winter Park. After the official formalities some of the dignitaries strolled through the Garden, led by Hamilton Holt and Edwin Grover, and viewed the orchids blooming in the Porter greenhouse, but most of the garden was just lush foliage and bursting buds that heralded the promise of things to come. It would be a few more months and some spring rain before the azaleas and camellias were in full bloom and the annuals, hyacinths, and tulips were producing great splashes of color.

8.8: *Dr. James West, national chief executive of the Boy Scouts of America, planting a cedar evergreen tree in Mead Botanical Garden, close to the Orlando entrance, on January 31, 1940. Grover and Connery are in the middle of the right-hand group.*

In the early months new plants arrived almost daily, sometimes as large collections but also as individual gifts. A rare Franklin Tree, a species first discovered on the banks of the Altamaha River by William Bartram, was received from the Bartram Association of Florida in commemoration of the 200th anniversary of his birth. The president of the association, Mrs. Millar Wilson of Jacksonville, presented it to Hamilton Holt, and it was planted close to the Winter Park entrance where it flowered profusely with large white flowers with yellow centers. The Boy Scouts of America contributed a cedar evergreen tree that was planted near the Orlando entrance by the organization's national chief executive, Dr. James West, with the idea that it could be lit as a Christmas tree for the holiday seasons.

Overall, Jack Connery and Edwin Grover were in an upbeat mood. In the early years they did not realize how much work was involved in converting the almost fifty acres of jungle and swampland into a garden. Now they had succeeded against substantial odds with the pivotal help of Martin Andersen who had relentlessly promoted the Garden through the pages of his newspaper and raised money for its opening. Edwin Grover had played a significant part too, smoothing over politics with the city, presenting endlessly a vision of the Garden to business leaders, and writing dozens of newspaper articles to publicize the Garden. And ably supporting these major efforts was Helen Connery, a tireless worker and skilled author, who had written several articles publicizing Mead the man and how his botanical garden would likely inspire all who visited it.

With plant donations now pouring in, they all looked forward to welcoming hundreds of paying visitors. The elation that they felt proved to be short-lived, as a personal tragedy befell the Grover family in the early hours of the morning of March 5, 1940. Grover's son, Graham, was struck by a northbound Atlantic Coast Line passenger train at the South Denning Drive crossing in Winter Park, just a few steps from Mead Botanical Garden, and died instantly. Suicide was suspected and the death affected Jack particularly badly. Graham had worked at the Garden for the last two years, had boarded with the Connerys for some of that time, and appeared to be on the road to recovery from a previous nervous breakdown, a recovery attributed largely to his friendship with Jack and Helen.

Chapter 9

Difficult Times in the 1940s

The Connery clan of grown-up children was a tight-knit family group that returned to their parent's residence on a regular basis for social events or for longer periods in times of trouble. They got together whenever possible at events like Christmas and in 1940 this gathering was photographed in the garden at 719 Hayden Lane, with the parents surrounded by their offspring, in-laws and grandchildren.

By that time, the eldest son, Bill, had married Eva Mary Bexley of Jacksonville in 1927, but divorced in 1937 and returned to photographic duties in the Orlando family business, joining his two younger brothers Joe and Charlie. The Connery's second son, Tom, had married Grace Brechin of Bergen, New Jersey, in 1930 and by 1940 they had produced four children, Malcolm (8), the twins Ronald and Donald (7), and Robert (2). Also in the photograph was Thelma Connery and her first husband photographer Bill Reynolds, and Jack and Helen with their two boys, Jackie and Edwin. Jack is not his usually smiling self but is looking uncharacteristically serious, perhaps preoccupied with the poor nature of Helen's health and his family's financial state.

9.1: The Connery family, Christmas 1940, in the garden of 741 W. Colonial Drive, Orlando. Back row (L to R); Jack, Bill, Charlie, Bill Reynolds (Thelma's husband), Thelma, Joe, and Tom. Middle row; Helen, Jackie (John Jr.), Mrs. Viola Connery, Mr. Hone Connery, twin Donald, Robert, and Grace (Tom's wife). Front row; Edwin, Malcolm, and twin Ronald.

In June 1941, Jack and Helen were fed up with renting and with the help of some family money bought property in Virginia Heights, Winter Park at 1358 Richmond Road, moving into the house in September. The Dinky Line* ran past the bottom of their garden and Jack would frequently take that route and walk to the Orlando Beverley Shores flag stop and into Mead Garden. To supplement the small income Jack received from Garden duties, Helen became part-time personal secretary to Edwin Grover, who had been appointed vice-president at Rollins College in 1938. Although both had given many years to the development of the Garden, it was not yet financially secure and able to allow Jack and Helen

---

* The Orlando and Winter Park railway that passed through the Rollins College campus on its way to Oviedo, and was nicknamed the Dinky Line by the students.

to take a decent living wage. Working long hours for little money took its toll, particularly on Helen, who became ill and had to be briefly hospitalized with malnutrition, exacerbated by the stress of living hand-to-mouth and looking after two young children. Dr. Gartley, who attended her, told Jack that it would be unwise for either of them to return to working at the Garden, and he needed to get a proper job.

Jack had proved to be an inspiring leader of the WPA workers at Mead Botanical Garden and was still loosely connected to the Garden as Director on Leave, but when he heard that they wanted someone to supervise a landscaping project at the nearby Orlando Air Base, which would be WPA-funded, he jumped at the chance to be considered. Opened in 1928 as the Orlando Municipal Airport, it was the first commercial airport in Central Florida, but was taken over by the US Army Air Corps in 1940 for use as a training facility and a center for fighter plane activities in anticipation of any outbreak of hostilities. Apart from a few airport buildings and a runway, most of the 60-acre site was wasteland, a palmetto scrub dotted with a few pines and bordered by a cypress swamp and described as only fit for a cow pasture. With Jack's experience in managing a large group of WPA-paid laborers in the task of landscaping and beautifying a large tract of Florida, and his knowledge and skills in palm tree planting, he got the job.

The plan was for the base to accommodate 350 officers and their families, as well as 2,000 or more enlisted men under the command of Colonel Thomas S. Voss, housed in fifty-seven new buildings of which thirty-three would be barracks for the enrolled men. An initial WPA grant of $271,719 was granted for the clearing and grubbing of land, construction of runways, erection of buildings and installation of sewer lines and a water system. A separate grant of $176,000 for landscaping and the erection of a wire fence to enclose the entire base was granted in early 1941, and on the morning of March 18 the huge landscaping project commenced under Jack's supervision.

Throughout the rest of 1941, enough rich loam was hauled onto the base to spread a four-inch thickness of top-soil into which tens of thousands of sprigs of Bermuda grass were planted. Over 16,000 cabbage palmetto trees were dug up along the St. Johns River and resettled across the site. In addition, thousands of potted plants and flower and hedge shrubbery cuttings were acquired from across Central Florida as gifts from generous citizens. Helping him with these tasks were not only the WPA workforce but dozens of 16 to 25-year-old youth workers from the National Youth Administration (NYA), a parallel New Deal employment organization to the WPA. Jack was in his element with this large workforce: he knew many of the WPA workers from the Mead Botanical Garden days and was an effective motivator of the youth workers through infectious enthusiasm and his experiences as a scout leader.

9.2: The main entrance of the US Army Air Base, Orlando looking north, showing the new buildings, paved streets, sidewalks, and Jack Connery's signature palm trees.

On Army Day, April 6, 1942, the center was open to visitors who were amazed at the transformation. The semi-wasteland had given way to a level, well-drained army base with orderly rows of neat white barrack buildings, paved streets and sidewalks replacing the sandy paths. Jack's signature palm trees were everywhere and a healthy growth of Bermuda grass carpeted the area, with trim hedges and flowering vines. A newspaper report of the day listed the people credited with the beautification work, ending with "…and last but not least, to Jack Connery, the man who developed Mead Botanical Garden and served as landscape engineer."

There was one last task before the facility could be fully operational and that was to camouflage the runways so that they could not be easily seen from the skies. Their linearity and reflectivity could be disguised by spreading them with a dark substance such as peat, and the army secured samples from various local suppliers. Jack decided that since there were large areas of peat either side of Howell Creek at Mead Botanical Garden, he would include a sample for comparison. The Garden peat was the winner and Jack negotiated with the base commander that they could take as much as they liked from the Garden so long as it was taken out under his supervision in the way he wanted. Over the summer of 1942, the army dug out 7,500 cubic yards of peat, and in exchange the Garden acquired two large lakes of an irregular and natural shape, from ten to fourteen feet deep and 200 to 300 feet long. The two lakes transformed the layout of the Garden, introducing larger areas of water to balance out the tropical plantings and allowing the display of tropical water lilies, including blue, pink, yellow and white varieties.

These were difficult times financially for the Connery family and following his work for the Airbase in Orlando, Jack looked around for other local horticultural opportunities to supplement their income. Entry into the war seemed inevitable, and the US government was seeking land for agricultural purposes to assist in providing food to troops during any conflict. The north shore of Lake Apopka, the state's fourth-largest lake located in Central Florida, became a desired location and a retention bank was built along the north shore to drain the shallow filtering marshlands and create 20,000 acres suitable for vegetable muck farms.

The area, part of Zellwood, fast became the new center for vegetable production in Central Florida. Jack found a job supporting the war effort on one of the farms and began growing Irish potatoes, carrots, beets, and beans. On one occasion, he took a sackful of potatoes into the local newspaper offices and handed them out for people to try. It was there that he admitted to having been given the nickname of Corncob Jack by the rest of the Zellwood farmers. On another occasion, he and Jim Wysong produced some beets weighing around five pounds apiece and carrots measuring ten inches in length that ended up on display at the offices of the County Agricultural agent. The agent explained that the giant vegetables were there as a marketing stunt for the fertile Zellwood farming district, but they were perfectly edible and not at all tough when eaten.

9.3: Brown Landone was an Influential New Thought and metaphysical leader and a prolific writer, authoring more than 100 books. He was a promoter of the Asian Shrub, ramie, as a fiber for textiles and inspired Jack to start growing it.

At Zellwood, Jack came across Dr. Brown Landone, an early leader of the New Thought Movement and Winter Park resident, who had a 180-acre experimental farm in Zellwood growing ramie, a plant that was a source of natural strong fibers suitable for use in textiles. Landone was a very persuasive figure and in late 1942 had called a meeting of business leaders and other interested parties to hear the story of ramie in his home at 837 Antonette Avenue in Winter Park. The audience listened as ramie was touted as the next big thing. It would grow easily and well in Florida and the sticking point up to now had been the absence of a mechanized machine to separate clean unbroken fibers from the cut green plant. Now after three years of research, and the examination of numerous alternative processes, Landone had invented a new machine to do that job, a process called decorticating. The machine was neither complicated nor costly and the process took only five hours to extract the cleaned, undamaged long fibers demanded by the textile industry from the growing plant in the field. According to Landone, nothing now stood in the way of Florida becoming an extensive producer of ramie. The prophet was heralding a new wonder crop that had the potential to make all his followers extremely rich. As a result, many investors rushed to put money into growing ramie either on land they already had or by buying land specifically for that purpose.

Landone's meeting was held but a few blocks from Jack's house and it is not known whether or not Jack attended and heard the sales pitch. But it would seem highly likely because in 1945, Jack secured a job as Plantation Superintendent managing 1,500 acres of ramie for the Florida Ramie Products Corporation in south-east Florida. The company was leasing the land from State Prison Farm No. 2 at Belle Glade, and Jack moved the family to nearby Lake Worth, buying a home at 1602 S. Lakeside Drive.

Initially the farm used converted hemp harvesters to crop the ramie for animal feed, where the green stalks and leaves were ground into meal at the main plant and dried in a mechanical dryer, then shipped to feed manufacturers to be mixed with other ingredients. Meanwhile, under Jack's direction, work went on converting one of the hemp harvesters to cut and bind fully grown ramie stalks for further processing into fiber. Despite the speculative promises of Brown Landone, decorticating the stalks to remove the inner fiber bundle and then degumming the bundle chemically to separate the individual fibers, still remained labor-intensive processes. The allure of the unbreakable ramie remained strong however and when Edwin Grover visited the Connerys and toured the facility, he described the experience to Hamilton Holt back at Rollins College in a letter, enclosing a piece of ramie fiber which he dared Holt to try to break.

9.4: Jack looking after his ramie crop in one of the Florida Ramie Products Corporation's fields, near Belle Glade, Florida, circa 1946.

Jack had been appointed scoutmaster to Troop 59 in Winter Park in 1938 but had to resign that position with the move to Lake Worth. There he remained committed to the scout movement and became involved with the cub and scout troops in the area. Meetings occasionally took place at the Connery home and as a senior scout he generally led the group singing at closing time. Both his sons started as cub scouts and in October 1947, Jackie graduated from Pack 7 and Edwin received his Cub Scout service star.

The Connery home was close to the ocean, and his time with William Beebe on Nonsuch Island had earned him the Captain Jack nickname, so when there was a proposal in the Lake Worth area to form a unit of Sea Scouts, Ship 3, Jack volunteered to be skipper. The group visited the US Coast Guard station at Lake Worth Inlet, and in April 1946, were entertained on a Sunday deep-sea fishing trip aboard R. L. Coleman's yacht *Lucky*. The all-day cruise began at 9:30 a.m. and extended to 6 p.m., with successful results although Jack reported that unsurprisingly none of the fish caught were large enough to be entered in the West Palm Beach Sailfish Derby.

9.5: Skipper Jack with his troop of Ship 3 Sea Scouts at Lake Worth, circa 1946.

Jack boated and fished on the inland waterways, lakes and canals around Lake Worth, and was bothered by the increasing amounts of floating weeds – principally water hyacinth – that occasionally blocked waterways and limited boat traffic. In some areas it produced a dense canopy at the water surface that boosted mosquito numbers and depleted the water of dissolved oxygen, effectively suffocating the fish.

The floating water hyacinth was introduced into Florida in the 1880s and initially it was intentionally planted in ponds and lakes where it was admired for its large spikes of lavender-blue flowers. It spread slowly at first, but with the boom in population and urban development following WWII, when rivers were dammed, wetlands drained, and nutrient-rich waters created by uncontrolled sewage releases and fertilizer runoff, the stage was set for an explosion of aggressive growth, and by the mid-1940s water hyacinth growth had become a serious problem.

9.6: *Water hyacinth was a troublesome invasive floating weed on Florida lakes and waterways. Jack developed a borax-containing spray that completely disintegrated the weed.*

Initially control centered on mechanical removal, but Jack saw how inefficient this process was and began to experiment with some of the chemical cocktails he was familiar with from his days in the Brogden laboratories, particularly formulations containing borax. He came up with a spray that completely disintegrated the hyacinth. He tried it out on some bathing beaches around midland lakes just north of Lake Worth that had become choked with the floating weed. He made a presentation of its effects before the Palm Beach County Resources and Development Board, claiming that the chemical spray destroyed the plants quickly and was not harmful to cattle. However, the Board told him that although successful in killing the invasive weed, the borax component ran afoul of Florida State law that banned the use of poison in sprays. Subsequently effective herbicides were developed to contain the water hyacinth but it continues to be a problem, particularly in Southern Florida where it grows year-round.

Many interested investors and speculators visited Jack at the Belle Glade ramie farm. In 1948, one of them was an agent representing Jose Manuel Aleman, a Cuban State official who was looking to grow ramie on half a dozen farms on the island. The agent explained that the objective was to diversify Cuban agriculture, then almost exclusively devoted to sugar cane. The climate in Cuba was suitable for possibly four ramie crops per year, rather than two as in the southern states. He indicated that Aleman also knew of a company keen to plant a million acres in Cuba and, if successful, would erect a textile plant there to supply ramie cloth to the South American market.

Jose Aleman was the Minister of Education for Cuba and a colorful character, only four years older than Jack but already a Cuban millionaire with extensive investments in ranches and property in Cuba and the Miami area. He rose to power during 1946 under President Roman Grau San Martin, who controlled most of the political patronage of the island, and who made him Minister of Education. At that time, there was rampant corruption in Cuba and public officials at all levels in government lived off bribery, payoffs and fixes. According to Harry Taber, general manager of Aleman's corporations and in charge of his business affairs in the US, he had invested over $15M in south Florida which included ownership of the Miami Sun Sox minor league baseball team. There were many who thought that this was a dramatic underestimate and that his total holdings were more in the range of $70M to $200M. How he had managed to invest this amount of money in the Miami area on his relatively modest salary as a Cuban minister was a mystery to only a few, and the popular view was that Aleman's ministerial promotion allowed him free reign to misappropriate vast quantities of government funds for his own benefit, particularly since it was known that he was in charge of all currency movements in and out of the Cuban National Treasury.

Just before Christmas 1948, Jack and the family moved to Havana to begin a five-year contract on January 1, 1949 as an agricultural engineer at a salary of $7,000 a year that he had orally agreed with Aleman. A suite of rooms was arranged by Aleman for them at The Royal Palm Hotel in Vedado, until they could find suitable rented accommodation in Havana.

The move to Havana was fortunate in some ways because in August 1949, only eight months after he left Florida, a Category 4 hurricane struck the coast near Lake Worth, moving inland with very high winds and dumping torrents of rain. The area had suffered a major hurricane before in September 1947 that had inflicted significant flooding and crop damage at the farm, but no significant loss of structural facilities nor equipment. This time it was different, and the Belle Glade prison farm and the Florida Ramie Products Corporation factory were directly in the hurricane's path and were badly damaged. Wind speeds reached a reported 175 mph in gusts, causing several roofs to be blown off and a shed to collapse on top of $50,000 worth of trucks, tractors and farm implements. Torrential rain caused extensive flooding and crop damage and the ramie processing plant was abandoned, eventually being taken over by the state and used for experimental studies of the recycling of waste vegetables for livestock feed.

In 1949, Jack had turned forty and was enjoying the good life in Havana with a higher salary relative to most workers on the island. The family was in Cuba for less than two years and not many details exist of their time there. At one point Jack flew to Texas in order to purchase livestock, visiting the King Ranch, near Kingsville, to buy Santa Gertrudis beef cattle for breeding purposes on one of Aleman's many Cuban ranches. Helen was active in the garden section of the Havana Woman's Club and organized several flower shows. Unfortunately in

March 1950, after a long illness, Jose Aleman died of cancer aged forty-five at his home in Kohly, a Havana suburb, and with the death of his benefactor, Jack was out of a job.

Aleman had spent much of the previous two years receiving medical treatment for his condition in Miami, where his major property and business interests were. The Connerys returned to Miami, where Jack found work at a landscaping company and tried to obtain financial compensation for his job loss through the Dade Circuit court. In January 1951, he sued the Aleman Estate for $35,441, citing his five-year oral contract commencing January 1, 1949 at $7,000 a year and his wrongful dismissal on April 1, 1950. No record of the verdict could be found but it would seem unlikely that it succeeded.

Chapter 10

The DeLand Years

Jack's younger brother Joe, who worked with him on the Mead Botanical Garden project, had at the age of thirty-four met and married Rena Caroline Dyer, an English lady of Lancastrian descent who was living with her family in DeLand, a city forty miles or so north of Orlando. The married couple had made their home at 411 W. Howry Avenue. Joe's father-in-law, Leslie Dyer, operated an outboard and marine shop at 111 W. Indiana Avenue and following his daughter's wedding to Joe helped set up the Dyer-Connery photographic studio at 222 N. Woodland Blvd. Jack and Joe were very close as brothers and so it was to DeLand that Jack and the family moved to from Miami in late 1951, enrolling the two boys in DeLand High School.

Jack had plenty of landscaping knowledge and both he and Helen were by now experienced horticulturists, so they decided to start a nursery and landscaping business, naming it after Helen's childhood nickname of Mimi. They bought residential property at 1100 Stevens Avenue and acquired the best part of a city block nearby at 1180 Talton Avenue on which to establish the greenhouses and other production and growing areas. Initially Mimi's Nursery & Landscape concentrated on a wide range of semi-tropical flowering and foliage plants, such as crotons, philodendrons, poinsettias and rex begonias, before their business focus changed to emphasize flowering plants like camellias, azaleas and gloxinias, which they found were easier to sell. Not surprisingly, following her exposure to the plants of Theodore Mead, Helen had developed a keen interest in orchids and had an extensive collection. She was also growing saintpaulias or African violets as a hobby and had become expert in their culture and propagation.

10.1: Top: A display for Mimi's Nursery & Landscape, dated February 11, 1953. Bottom: A later display showing the shift from largely foliage plants to flowering ones, such as camellias and gloxinias.

Horticulture featured high on their list of social activities in DeLand too, with Helen appointed President of the Garden Club and organizer and chairman of the annual flower show, positions she held for several years. Jack helped out at the flower show, heading up the horticultural committee. He was busy with the nursery plants and always on the lookout for landscaping jobs. One came his way in early 1953 at nearby DeLeon Springs, nine miles north of DeLand on US Hwy 17, which was undergoing significant remodeling and relandscaping as a tourist roadside attraction based on the Spanish explorer Juan Ponce de León and the mythological Fountain of Youth.

10.2: A jungle cruise through many small islands was a feature of the Ponce de Leon Springs, just one of the many tourist road-side attractions in Florida claiming a connection to the early Spanish explorers and the famed fountain of youth. At the entrance to the springs was a statue featuring a Spanish conquistador (right).

The landscaping job involved creating flower gardens and planting palms, camellias and other semi-tropical flowering plants, all as a backdrop to a jungle cruise attraction in an electric-powered boat that twisted and turned through fourteen small islands each planted with lush tropical foliage. On one island there was a collection of monkeys with their keeper, on others a tropical bird or various tame animals imported from South America, Australia, Africa and

Asia. Apart from the jungle cruise, visitors could visit a wild animal compound or take a rejuvenating swim in its Fountain of Youth. On May 29, 1953, the newly transformed Ponce de Leon Springs opened to the general public who were drawn into the attraction by the sight at the entrance to the springs of a nine-foot-high replica of a Spanish conquistador, with a bathing-beauty statue on his arm.

In the early 1950s, Jack and Helen still had a connection with Mead Botanical Garden. Helen was elected secretary in 1952 and in December of that year Jack Connery and Edwin Grover signed away all rights to the $23,000 they had initially lent the Garden, allowing it to become debt-free. Jack visited the Garden when he could, spent time with Grover, and organized groups of volunteers to help with cleaning and clearing up. For several summers, Jack and his son Edwin worked with Mac McConnell, the chief caretaker at the Garden, repotting, fertilizing and generally looking after the orchids in the greenhouses. Edwin Connery recalled that period spent tending the orchids and spoke of the difficulty in keeping the collection together with virtually no control on access to the greenhouses. Locals, volunteers, and sometimes visitors were in the habit of taking any plant they took a fancy to, and Edwin recalls this as a real problem. He remembers his father summing it up with the wry comment that "many a person's orchid collection was started with (free) orchids from Mead Garden." But Edwin's most persistent memory of that time was the monotony of the lunch menu. Mac was a vegetarian and every day they ate the same thing – white bread sandwiches spread with peanut butter and honey.

Apart from the orchids that were on permanent display, Mead Garden held various annual flower shows in the 1940s and 1950s. Daylilies, amaryllis, camellias, hibiscus, and begonias were featured and the events attracted thousands of people and influenced some to start their own individual plant collections. Attending the first annual Central Florida Hibiscus Show on Sunday, June 24, 1951, happened to be one of the Connery family, Jack's sister Thelma. She was taken with the brilliant scarlet, saffron, yellow and white blooms of this plant, a native to China and known as the queen of tropical flowers, and bought several plants at the show and started growing them.

Thelma was married to her second husband, Steven Johnson, and in 1950 they had bought the cottage at 719 Hayden Lane to be near Thelma's aging parents. Following the loss of her mother, Viola, they acquired the rest of the property and the big house at 741 W. Colonial Drive in 1953, where they tended for Thelma's father, Hone Connery, until he too passed away in September 1954, aged seventy-seven.

10.3: *Suzy Johnson with her prize-winning yellow and peach double hibiscus hybrid that she named after her mother, Viola Connery.*

Steven and Suzy Johnson – her husband preferred to call her Suzy rather than Thelma – enthusiastically took up hibiscus cultivation and started to grow and hybridize them as a hobby. On most Sundays over the summer, they spent their time travelling and exhibiting their creations at state and local shows, and became adept hybridizers, frequently winning awards. In 1957, Suzy won top honors for her new yellow and peach double variety, which she named after her mother, Viola Connery.

A single blossom with similar colors she named after her aunt, Adeline Brogden. In turn, Steven Johnson had several best-in-show awards, one for his Ruffled Beauty, a toned orange single-bloom hibiscus.

The couple ended up developing a collection of 850 named varieties plus more than 2,500 seedlings in the open garden of the Colonial Drive property. The big house remained a center for Connery family get-togethers, and no doubt Jack and Helen exchanged horticultural experiences with the Johnsons when they visited. Unfortunately, a devastating overnight freeze in 1962 killed all unprotected hibiscus plants in the Central Florida area and quickly deflated the Johnsons' enthusiasm for their culture.

Meanwhile Jack was still looking for horticulturally-related get-rich opportunities. The ramie boom that he had been part of in Florida had burst and investors had lost their shirts, largely because processing mechanization had not been available to economically separate the long continuous ramie fibers suitable for textile spinning. But Jack still had the dream of becoming a wealthy fiber king, an idea sold to him by Brown Landone, and discovered an alternative plant in kenaf, *hibiscus cannabinus*. Like ramie, together with flax, hemp and jute, the fibers of kenaf came from the pithy part of the plant stem and were made up of both long and short fibers, ideally suited as pulp for high-quality paper production and therefore an alternative to wood-pulp from trees. Jack, like others, became a promoter of the new wonder plant and featured his vision in an Orlando newspaper headlined "DeLand man plans wealth from kenaf."

According to Jack, and as reported in the newspaper, all that was needed to start was $150,000 for the decorticating machine, 3,000 acres of land for growing, and 90 days of waiting for the plant to be ready to harvest. The article then described Jack scribbling speculative figures for growing costs, selling prices and yields per acre on a piece of paper before declaring the potential for wealth generation to be 'fantastic'. Jack could be prone to exaggeration on occasion and this flight of fancy was an example where he got carried away with the numbers. But once again speculators carried the day, and kenaf planting commenced in Florida centered around the Vero Beach area. What came next was just bad luck and not related to Jack's enthusiastic promotion, but to the condition and purity of the kenaf seed.

The Miami News of May 24, 1953 summed up the problem with the headline "Promising Florida crop near death unless new research can rescue it." The first problem was an extensive fungal infection on 1,800 acres of kenaf being grown for seed near Vero Beach. The disease ruined many growers and emphasized the need to treat the seed with fungicide before planting and, for the long term, hope for the development of a more disease-resistant kenaf variety. The second problem that hit the growers in that area of Florida was beautiful to look at but devastating from a commercial point of view.

Over the summer of 1952, the American Kenaf and Ramie Corporation planted 2,700 acres for fiber production, and at harvest time the kenaf fields looked beautiful. The fields were ablaze with morning glory vines that entwined themselves on every kenaf fiber stalk in the fields. When harvesters moved into the rows, the vines tangled in the combine blades, wrapped themselves around the running gear, bogged down the machines and brought harvesting to a halt. The seed of the morning glory and that of kenaf are similar in size, color and shape and somehow accidental mixing of the two seemed to have happened. The conclusion was that for kenaf growing to make a comeback, a disease resistant kenaf variety and a way of separating kenaf seeds from similar others needed to be found. Once again, just like ramie, investors betting on getting rich quick jumped too early on the kenaf bandwagon only to lose everything.

More steady income for Jack came from his growing experience of running nursery operations and the associated landscaping contracts that frequently came with them. In April 1955, he was called in to liquidate the stock at the Silver Springs Nursery, just off Lemon Avenue in Ocala, due to the death of owner Frank Mitchell. The nursery was the principal supplier of plants to the nearby Ponce de Leon Springs, and large collections of azaleas, camellias, and hydrangeas were offered at give-away prices. With a housing boom in full swing, Jack hit on the idea of providing comprehensive plant assortments for owners of new homes, stating "$35 will buy a truckload of plants." The sale closed a month later and the balance of the unsold plants, mainly camellias, transferred to Mimi's Nursery in DeLand, where they were advertised in the local paper. Following this, Jack was employed running the Ocala Garden Mart on S. Pine Street in Ocala, offering free advice and estimates on landscaping and a full range of garden plants, peat, fertilizers, topsoil, gardening tools and equipment.

10.4: Jack was called in to liquidate the stock at the Silver Springs Nursery, Ocala, due to the death of owner Frank Mitchell. The nursery was the principal supplier of plants to the nearby Ponce de Leon Springs and unsold stock ended up at Mimi's.

Both Helen and Jack continued to be active in the local horticultural scene, giving talks on growing annuals or on Helen's favorite flower, the African violet. Their approach was always practical and helpful and they readily shared their experiences, particularly for the African violet that some found difficult to grow.

At the talks, Helen would present in great detail her formula gathered through years of experience in the growth and development of the 10,000 violets she had in her collection. She stressed the point that 90% of the problems encountered were due to over-watering, because a plant would likely recover from lack of water but not from too much of it. Because of the humid Florida climate, she favored top-watering African violets and watering late in the evening to prevent leaf spotting caused by sun on wet leaves. Jack suggested the 'feel of the soil' method as a guide for watering; when soil pinched between the fingers no longer adhered together, it was time for watering. According to Jack, in Florida this would typically be from one to three times a week, so the soil is kept damp but not flooded. As well as her presidency of the DeLand Garden Club, Helen also served as chairman of landscape design for the Florida Federation of Garden Clubs and received an award in that field from the National Council of State Garden Clubs at its Miami convention in 1957.

10.5: Helen and Jack Connery were enthusiastic and passionate communicators in all matters horticultural, especially related to the growing of African violets. Picture dated June 1955.

Chapter 11

The African Violet Business

By the mid to late 1950s, a commercial decision was made to have the nursery operations concentrate solely on the propagation and cultivation of the African violet, which had the advantage of being a small, inexpensive plant, available in many floral colors. It was the perfect miniature windowsill plant, a symbol of loyalty, devotion, and faithfulness, and a popular purchase around Mother's Day, Easter and Valentine's Day. From a horticultural point-of-view, tens of thousands could be grown in relatively small greenhouses and cultivar creation and propagation was straightforward. Cultivars for commercial production could be selected for consistent growth, uniform flowering, and trueness to type, and from a sales point of view chosen to provide customers with a wide variety of flower colors and cultivar selection to maintain interest throughout the year. As growing them became more popular, cultivar proliferation resulted in hundreds of new varieties with names such as Frost and Flame, Dazzling Deceiver, Fashion Frenzy, and Creekside Moonbeams. Cultivars registered to the Connerys were named in a little more restrained manner; Mimi's Blushing Pink, Mimi's Master Jack, and Mimi's Perfect Delight were some examples.

11.1: The Connery's decided to concentrate on the growing of African violets whose bright flowers and multiple colors along with their velvety, evergreen leaves made them consumer favorites.

Setting up a new nursery business in Central Florida was not without its difficulties due to the vagaries of the weather. Although direct hurricane activity was rare, storms and precipitous rainfall were not. In October 1956 a tropical storm passed northwards through Central Florida, dumping inches of rain and causing extensive flooding. The worse hit area was Kissimmee with almost fourteen inches of rain in one day on October 16; by the end of the day on October 17 DeLand had received five to seven inches in total and Mimi's nursery was under water, with many plants ruined. The Connerys applied for a small-business Disaster Loan from the federal government and were granted $3,250 in 1957 in order to rebuild stock and repair damage to buildings.

Despite this setback, by around 1960 the nursery had established a strong reputation in the quality and variety of its African violets and was looking to expand the business. With more than five years' experience in their commercial growing, and four greenhouses on the Talton Avenue site, they were capable of producing annually up to a million violets. Around this time, the F. W. Woolworth

Company placed a contract with the nursery to provide them with 10,000 African violets a month across their regional stores. Included was the expertise of Helen and Jack, who would attend key Woolworth stores and give talks on how to grow and look after the plants, detailing such things as proper watering and fertilizing, the role of lighting in promoting growth, and recommended sprays and types of pot. This would be followed by a Q&A session. As an aid to selling, they would be provided with space to assemble an attractive presentation of as many different types of violets as possible to compliment the store's display, and local newspapers would advertise the events and invite local garden club members and interested parties to attend.

11.2: The F. W. Woolworth Company placed a contract with Mimi's nursery to provide them with 10,000 African violets a month across their regional stores.

The first mention of a Connery African violet display, lecture and clinic in a Woolworth store that has been found appeared in the Fort Pierce News-Tribune newspaper of Monday, November 20, 1961. It promised the talk would commence at 10 a.m. on Tuesday, attendees would see more than twenty-two different types of violets that would also be offered for sale, and the lecture would be free of charge. Following the success of the Fort Pierce experiment,

Woolworth went ahead in 1962 with much larger trials at stores on the east coast of Southern Florida, from West Palm Beach to Miami, with the Cypress Plaza store in Pompano Beach and the Sunrise Shopping Center and Downtown stores in Fort Lauderdale being prime locations.

11.3: *A selection of Woolworth newspaper advertisements for the special events where Jack and Helen Connery would conduct plant clinics promoting African violets and sharing their experience of their care and culture.*

Now they were running a real business, the organizational skills of Helen came to the fore, and she took care of all aspects of accounting, invoicing, and scheduling deliveries to Woolworth, while Jack looked after the economics of commercial growing and operational management of the greenhouses. Helen wrote everything down in great detail concerning the optimum growing conditions of lighting, temperature, humidity, and watering, so that when they were away from DeLand selling and marketing the plants, things could continue at a smooth pace in the greenhouses. Jack's two sons were initially assistant managers of the business, and their wives and several young girls from the DeLand community were employed to help with greenhouse operations.

The production of large quantities of African violets involved propagation by leaf cuttings, then preserving valuable greenhouse space by transplanting the plug-grown rooted plantlets into 2-inch pots to maximize production across the greenhouses. The objective was to produce plants with healthy attractive foliage and the start of flower stalks and indications of buds for shipment to Woolworth. To control growth and budding, Jack turned to the provision of artificial lighting to supplement the natural daylight in the greenhouses, fitting fluorescent lights under bench areas in one of the greenhouses to make it more productive. He built two separate smaller fiberboard sheds with no natural light and only overhanging fluorescent grow lights designed to emit the correct spectral colors to enhance growth and promote flowering. Jack wanted to understand how to get the best out of the lighting set-up he was using and was curious as to whether different varieties of violets responded differently to lighting, using the yardstick of the average time to flowering in days. He needed someone to research these topics and turned to the local high school for help.

The exotically-named Tribble J. Dicks was a teacher of biology and anatomy in the Department of Science at DeLand High School, having received a Bachelor of Science degree in biology from Stetson University in 1962. A retired US navy commander in his late forties, he was looking to continue his academic work with a Master of Science degree, encouraged by his Stetson supervisor Dr. E. C. Prichard. In consultation with the Connerys, and their full support, he undertook to investigate the effects of artificial lighting under the thesis title "The Effects of Fluorescent Light on Growth and Flowering of Saintpaulias." The work took place over the years 1963 to 1965 using Mimi's greenhouses and nursery as experimental facilities, and Dicks was awarded a Master of Science degree from Stetson University in 1966. The Connerys were generous in sharing the findings of this research with the African violet community and the details were published in the *African Violet Magazine* in five parts covering the issues June 1968 to March 1969. The work was well-received and judged a useful contribution to the subject.

Throughout 1963 and 1964, the Connerys remained busy supporting the Fort Lauderdale Woolworth stores, with attendance dates in March, April, June, October, November and December. During 1965, they were asked by Woolworth to present the violet clinic outside their home state of Florida, appearing in April in a store in Raleigh, North Carolina and during August in Hattiesburg, Mississippi, selling violets at two for 88 cents. The journey to North Carolina offered Jack the opportunity to call in and see his brother, Tom, living in nearby Durham and suffering from a long-term illness caused by a stroke he had had in 1954, and this trip became an Eastertime tradition for the next couple of years.

The period 1966 to 1970 was the busiest for the Connerys in terms of fulfilling the contract with Woolworth. 1966 started off with an extended stay throughout January in the St. Petersburg/Fort Myers areas, appearing before local garden clubs as well as Woolworth, before returning to Miami. There was further expansion across the southern states and they visited Woolworth in Atlanta, Georgia in March. In April they attended the twentieth annual show and convention of the African Violet Society at the Americana Hotel, Bal Harbor, Miami Beach, that ran from April 13-15, with the theme "From the Everglades to the Sea." The week before the convention they had a display at the local Woolworth store with dense foliage materials, nautical-related objects and small potted plants, all surrounding a central silver tray featuring fresh blossoms from many familiar African violet varieties. At the convention, there was a commercial show area where the Connerys had a booth, and Woolworth donated the silver tray to present as a blue-ribbon award. Being helpful and sharing experiences with other delegates resulted in Helen and Jack earning the vote of 'most co-operative' at the show. For the last three months of 1966, they were once again in the Fort Myers and Fort Lauderdale Woolworth stores.

They took special care with the attractiveness of the displays in the Woolworth stores, echoing the theme of any local African violet show that was being held in the vicinity. In March 1967, they attended the African Violet Society of Miami's show, paralleling with a Woolworth display with the same theme of "Pathways to Beauty," for which they received an Award of Distinction. They were asked to go to Woolworth stores in Tennessee in June 1967 and then again in August, visiting Johnson City, Kingsport and Nashville, visits that were repeated in 1969 and 1970. Up to this point they had used a large station wagon fitted with shelves for the violets as their mode of transport but eventually they purchased a Winnebago recreational vehicle to give them more space and convenience for overnight stops.

11.4: At African violet shows and conventions, and in the Woolworth stores, the Connerys made sure their display booths were attractive and echoed the theme of the shows, in this case Hawaii as a dream vacation destination.

February 1969 had them again in Fort Lauderdale at the Hollywood Mall where the African Violet Society of Miami, the South Florida African Violet Club, and the Little River African Violet Club staged their combined show on long tables along the length of the mall. Guests came from many states as well as Canada and Jamaica, and the Connerys were awarded the title of 'best commercial display'. Helen was a member of the Dixie African Violet Society and attended their regular meetings with Jack when she could. In March 1969, they were present at the 13th Annual Convention and Show at the Jack Tar Hotel in Baton Rouge, Mississippi. At the Friday night awards banquet, in honor of the convention, they gave each of the 125 delegates one of their own hybridizations, "Miss Baton Rouge," a shell pink, double bloom, semi-miniature variety that served as decoration on the tables at the dinner.

The business started to wind down with the start of the 1970s, although they remained regulars for the next few years at Cypress Plaza's Woolworth store in Pompano Beach. On Friday October 13, 1972, they ran separate clinics; Helen at Cypress Plaza and Jack in the nearby Fashion Square branch. Violets were by then 49c each and over 100 different varieties were on display. This appears to be the last date for a clinic hosted by the Connerys, although they still continued to supply Woolworth with violets.

Each violet that Woolworth sold had a label that indicated it had been shipped in from Florida's largest growers, Mimi's African Violets in DeLand, so the greenhouses there had become a destination for visits from local African violet societies in Florida. Jack and Helen were perfect hosts on these events, providing refreshments and generous help and advice. One society's visit report in 1973 stated that they were preparing some 4,000 plants for shipment when they arrived and that the girls who were doing the work were very friendly, which reflected well on the owners. Another visit from the Miracle Strip African Violet Society provoked the response "They were very gracious hosts to the club and when the motorcade arrived at their greenhouses, they had made elaborate luncheon preparations for the entire club membership. It was an amazing experience for the new members who had never seen such an array and display of African violets."

African violets became a thing of the past for Jack and Helen when they left the business in DeLand in 1975 and moved back to Orlando. It brought to an end over twenty years in their cultivation, fifteen years or so supplying Woolworth with plants, and eleven years conducting clinics in Woolworth stores throughout the South helping to bring African violet popularity to a mass market. No record of new owners of the DeLand nursery business has been found but one possibility was that the family were involved and continued it in some way. Evidence for this comes from advertisements in the late 1970s editions of *African Violet Magazine* for Mimi's African violet kits, and the fact that the DeLand nursery was still receiving visits from African violet societies right up to 1979.

11.5: The African Violet Magazine (left) was where the Connery's published their results on the effects of artificial light on the growth of violets and, in the late 1970s, marketed the sale of their starter kits (right).

But this was not the end of the connection between African violets and the Connery family. Jack's married sister, Suzy Johnson, had acquired a keen horticultural interest in the hibiscus family of plants during the 1950s but in the early 1960s shifted her focus to the cultivation of African violets, taking inspiration from her sister-in-law's business in DeLand. From the beginning, Helen had documented all that she and Jack had learned about the cultivation, propagation and hybridization of African violets and doubtless this information was passed on within the family to Suzy. She became an enthusiastic hobby-grower, installing a greenhouse, and establishing an African violet society in Haines City, south of Orlando. Her interest grew throughout the 1960s, as did the number of interested growers in the region, leading to the formation of the Central Florida African Violet Society in 1971, with Suzy as chairman. She became a prolific educator, teacher and radio/TV presenter on the subject in the 1980s.

Chapter 12

Closure

There are not many details of the closing years of Jack Connery's life. Assembling the small factual pieces into some sort of larger coherent picture is like being with Jack on one of his archaeological digs and discovering a few shards of certainty among mounds of speculation.

What we know is that Jack and Helen returned to Orlando in 1975, buying a single-family home with water views and canal access to Clear Lake at 2600 Windward Court on Catalina Island, paying $32,500 for the property. In the early 1970s, in anticipation of retirement, he had purchased a power boat in the form of the cuddy cabin Wellcraft Airslot that could be towed behind their Winnebago camper when they went on longer trips, and could be launched from the home directly into the canal. The Wellcraft was named *Miss Mimi Too* and a 1976 photograph captures Jack standing alongside the boat trailer behind the RV.

Jack's passion for fishing, a perfect companion to boating, was triggered when he was in his early teens with the arrival in the mail of a fishing rod and reel sent to him by his father. He was in his element when he had a rod in hand, fishing for snook at Hickory Pass near Bonita Springs or leisurely angling the St. Johns River at Blue Springs. We can imagine him enjoying the well-earned retirement years with Helen on boating and fishing trips across Central and Southern Florida, many involving overnight stopovers in the Winnebago or staying with friends and family. He was fortunate in having a loving and supportive wife who also liked to fish.

12.1: *In this 1976 photograph, Jack stands beside his Wellcraft Airslot power boat,* Miss Mimi Too, *towed by the Winnebago.*

Jack Connery's legacy for a biographer was a wealth of photographs and a handful of letters, the exact opposite of that of his horticultural and scouting mentor, Theodore Mead, who wrote and received three to four letters a week throughout his life and seemed to have kept them all. Without detailed letters, we can still piece Jack Connery's life story and personality together by augmenting the abundance of photographs with recollections of family members and newspaper accounts.

In terms of his personality, one of his aunts described him this way, "Jack was a quiet, kind, self-controlled person. At the same time, he was an engaging conversationalist and colorful storyteller. The details in his stories painted pictures of the events and escapades of his life. He lived life with exuberance."

A newspaper article from 1939 paints a similar picture, "Twenty-five years from now Jack may have long white whiskers, a bald head, and a dignified look. Today at the age of 30, he manifests so much driving energy, enthusiasm, personal warmth and friendliness, that even the children in the town call him Jack. He is Jack to all his workmen too." Certainly, many of the photographs of him show him happy and having fun. The other key attribute that comes through is generosity, a characteristic that he shared with Helen. An example of this was their horticultural knowledge and experience in African violet culture which they freely shared and passed on to Suzy Johnson, and Tribble's work on growth promotion using artificial light that was published for the benefit of the entire African violet community.

12.2: *A December 1961 photograph showing Helen and Jack's fishing tally for the day, with Jack holding his prize-winning striped bass.*

All his life Jack was in touch with the natural world, connecting with the disciplines of ornithology, marine biology, botany and archaeology. His first involvement was as a young Audubon Society member, joining the fight to stop the slaughter of Florida's birds for sport and their plume feathers. He captured his experiences with a camera, made lantern slides, and spent time communicating the beauty of bird life to others, hoping to awaken in them their own love of nature, a call that proved most powerful when he was talking to young people. In 1930, aged twenty-one, he went to Bermuda and experienced firsthand the wonder of the undersea world teeming with life, photographed some of the deep-sea creatures, and saw for himself their amazing bioluminescent features. As an Eagle Scout and through his friendship with scoutmaster Theodore Mead, he developed a deep love of the world of botany and learned about orchid culture and the horticulture of semi-tropical plants. During his time at Rollins College, he conducted archaeological excavations at Highlands Hammock, discovering a giant turtle fossil, and at Flagler Beach an arrowhead in close association with a jawbone of a mammoth, a discovery that challenged the existing theory of when and how North America was first settled. Finally, he returned to his first love of horticulture and grew tens of thousands of African violets, supplying the F. W. Woolworth stores and helping to popularize this pretty little plant.

Perhaps Jack's greatest legacy achievement was the physical creation of Mead Botanical Garden, work that was ably assisted by Helen and the astute yet unassuming Edwin Grover of Rollins College. In the early stages of the garden's founding, to hear Jack speak of the project would have been to witness an unbridled expression of joy and creativity. At that time, his youthful and hugely ambitious dream for the garden was for it to honor the three great naturalists who had shaped his life up to that time: Theodore Mead, Oscar Baynard, and William Beebe. To do this, he planned for visitors to experience the wide-ranging variety of the natural world; colorful semi-tropical plants and hundreds of rare and beautiful orchids housed in a huge greenhouse to honor Theodore Mead; exotic birds in an aviary spanning the creek in memory of Oscar Baynard; and, for William Beebe, exciting marine life in a purpose-built sea aquarium. The project exemplified Jack's visionary approach to horticulture and his desire to include other aspects of the natural world and bring these experiences to a wider audience. It demonstrated his ability to think big, an attribute that was carried over in later life to the establishment of Florida's largest commercial nursery for African violets.

12.3: Jack Connery's signature palm trees can still be seen at the Winter Park entrance to Mead Botanical Garden. Photograph taken 2019.

After enjoying several years of retirement, by 1978 old age had tightened its grip on Jack, and Helen was granted power of attorney over their affairs in July of that year. Four years later, aged 73, as the shadows lengthened across the lawn, he died from a cerebral hemorrhage and was buried in DeLand Memorial Gardens. Helen survived him by another eighteen years, dying in April 2000, aged 87.

There is little left of either Jack Connery or Theodore Mead's presence in today's Mead Botanical Garden, which is now a well-used community park. Mead's prize orchids and the greenhouses where they were displayed disappeared in the 1970s due to neglect and mismanagement but Jack's presence hangs on in a small grove of palm trees planted close to the Winter Park entrance.

For many years Jack resided in or close to Central Florida's Winter Park, and attended Rollins College. If there were to be a plaque recognizing his life, there could be no better one-line summary on it than "Jack Connery (1908-1982), Naturalist, the Rollins College student who left an indelible mark on the City of Winter Park."

Acknowledgments

Jack Connery was a photographer and came from a family in the business of photography. It is no surprise therefore in performing the research needed for this volume that most of the images come from the Connery family's own photographic collections. Hence my deepest thanks go to Edwin and Nancy Connery, and their daughter Cindy, for allowing me access to their respective treasure chests of photographs and negatives and for showing so much interest in getting the story of Jack and Helen Connery correctly documented. Wherever possible I've tried to use photographs where the subjects were identified and where dates are stated or can readily be estimated.

Most of the photographs were in their original black and white format as was the custom of the day. These have been brought to life in color as in the preceding two books. But instead of using the previous time-consuming practice of hand colorization via Photoshop, the images in this book have been automatically colorized with machine-learning algorithms from DeOldify, licensed to MyHeritage. The use of this technology is gratefully acknowledged.

Colorization of old photographs is a contentious issue. Some historians describe it as falsifying history. My position is that if done carefully, it is rewriting not falsifying history, making historical footage easier for new generations to digest.

In this exercise, nothing has been added to the original photograph apart from the color, and if the color is known to be wrong it has been changed via Photoshop adjustments.

Central to the full historical account of the life of Jack Connery were the articles published in archival versions of the Orlando Sentinel group of newspapers, available on newspapers.com. These form a major part of the book, and are the main source of research material spanning the years. It is no exaggeration to say that a volume of local history like this could not have been written without this information, and the effort involved in making these digitized accounts available is sincerely recognized.

I wish to acknowledge the assistance of Paul C. Palmer Jr., of Maitland, Florida for supplying me much information on the family history of the Englerths, who represent the blood line of Jack Connery's mother, née Viola Englerth. I am also indebted to Rollins College for allowing me access to the archival photographic collection of the Winter Park Garden Club. Also earning my warmest appreciation has to be proof-reader Nancy Davila, who provided valuable perspectives and frequent additions and suggested changes to the text. I also wish to thank Adam Harrower, of the Kirstenbosch Botanical Garden, Cape Town, South Africa, who was kind enough to allow me to use his photograph of the aerial walkway at the garden for the front and back cover. Finally, I am grateful to Jose at Pedernales Publishing who professionally executed the book formatting and put up with all my niggling little changes.

It is an unusual closing to thank a pandemic for a book's existence but, with forced time on my hands, it did allow the trilogy of documentation connected with Mead Botanical Garden to be completed.

Notes

Source Abbreviations

RC-TLM   The Theodore L. Mead Collection, Archives & Special Collections, Rollins College, Winter Park, Florida. A collection of 31 boxes of letters and other printed material, some diaries and a few photographs.

RC-WPGC   The Winter Park Garden Club Collection, Archives & Special Collections, Rollins College, Winter Park, Florida. A collection of 12 boxes of yearbooks, reports, newsletters and other printed material, some loose photographs and scrapbook images.

WPPL   Articles and material related to the Mead Botanical Garden, Winter Park Public Library, Winter Park, Florida.

WC   The Willis collection of private papers and photographs belonging to the Willis family, descendants of Theodore Mead's wife Edith, and housed in the ancestral Edwards home at Coalburg, West Virginia.

EC	The Edwin Connery and family collection. Personal communication with the son of Jack Connery and access to his collection of private papers and photographs at his home in Cape Coral, Florida. Additional photographs from Edwin's daughter, Cindy Connery Boone, living in Windermere, Florida.
ENG	Manuscript entitled "Our Englerth Family Heritage" by Nan J. Walker, detailing their family history that includes reference to Jack Connery's mother, born Viola Englerth, and references to Jack Connery's life. Unpublished manuscript provided by Paul C. Palmer Jr., Maitland, Florida.
AVM	The African Violet Magazine

Chapters four to six have been assembled largely from a range of information sources on William Beebe and his expeditions, particularly the first one involving bathysphere dives off Nonsuch Island in 1930 that included Jack Connery. His iconic photographs feature in many of the references. Readers wishing more information are referred to:

Wikipedia - https://en.wikipedia.org/wiki/William_Beebe.

The Official William Beebe Website - https://sites.google.com/site/cwilliambeebe/Home.

Carol Grant Gould, *The Remarkable Life of William Beebe* (Washington: Island Press, 2004).

Brad Matsen, *Descent: The Heroic Discovery of the Abyss* (New York: Knopf Doubleday Publishing Group, 2007).

William Beebe, *Half Mile Down* (New York: Harcourt, Brace & Co., 1934).

William Beebe, "A Round Trip to Davy Jones' Locker" *National Geographic*, June 1931.

William Beebe, "A Wonderer Under Sea" *National Geographic*, December 1932.

Robert Ballard and Will Hively, *The Eternal Darkness: A Personal History of Deep-Sea Exploration* (Princeton University Press, 2000).

There is some minor overlap in this book with the first two books of this trilogy when referencing Theodore Mead and the Mead Botanical Garden.

Paul Butler, *Orchids and Butterflies* (Little Red Hen Press, 2016).

Paul Butler, *Hope Springs Eternal* (Little Red Hen Press, 2019).

Also of interest might be Edwin Grover's biography by Eduard Gfeller, *The Business of Making Good*, 2016.

CHAPTER ONE

The early history of the Charles H. Connery family in America comes from Ancestry.com. It appears that he and William Hone, at the time a ship's captain, became related when they married the Hurd sisters, Louisa and Sarah, in Connecticut around 1844. The two families moved to Savannah around 1850 and William Hone gave up the sea and joined forces with Connery in the ship chandler business. The two families became closer when Charles Connery's eldest son, Charles Pentland Connery Sr., married William Hone's daughter, Anna S. Hone, in July 1874, and from this union William Hone Connery was born. Details of the Hone & Connery business comes from an obituary of William Hone in the Savannah newspaper ("An Old Citizen Gone," *The Morning News*, March 23, 1893).

The two sons of Charles and Anna Connery, Charles Pentland Jr. and William Hone, a year in age apart, became prolific cycle racers, with William going by the name of 'Hone Connery' as a differentiator. Their exploits made the local newspaper ("Thompson Beats Connery: Florida Crack Defeats the Savannah Rider Twice," *The Morning News*, July 17, 1898; "The Day with the Cyclers,"

The Morning News, April 26, 1899). At some of the meetings, Hone Connery entertained the crowd with a display of trick cycling ("A Race Meet to be Held at Thunderbolt Driving Park," *The Morning News*, May 15, 1898), but proved himself a fast racer at others ("Connery Wins the First Heat," *The Morning News*, September 6, 1898). The United States 1900 Federal Census lists Charles' occupation as bicycle repairer, and the 1897 Savannah City Directory records Hone Connery as a clerk at the Savannah Cycle Agency.

The 1902 volcanic eruption of Mt. Pelée was one of the worst volcanic disasters of the twentieth century – see https://en.wikipedia.org/wiki/1902_eruption_of_Mount_Pel%C3%A9e. Hone Connery departed for Cuba on May 18 (*Savannah Morning News*, May 18, 1902) and a full description of his trip on his return, including his reference to coining money, appeared as "Antilles Photo'D – Savannahian's Tour of Cuba and Porto Rico with Camera," *Savannah Morning News*, July 29, 1902.

Viola Englerth's courtship with Hone Connery is documented in ENG (Nan Walker's manuscript "Our Englerth Family Heritage"), and their wedding details, including sailing for Porto Rico, appears in the *Savannah Morning News* of December 23, 1902. The island's name of Puerto Rico was anglicized to Porto Rico by the United States in 1898 but changed back in 1931.

T. H. Payne was established in 1865 by Thomas Payne and Zeboim C. Patten as a small six-foot store selling books and stationery and moved to 823 Market Street in 1883; Chattanooga Memory Project (https://stories.chattanoogamemory.com/stories/1283). Hone Connery's progression from Harris & Hogshead, Optometrists and Manufacturing Opticians, to Austin Photo Supply Co., and then to the Connery Photo Supply Co., are traced in the Chattanooga City Directories of that time.

Jack Connery's legal birth certificate, indicating the name "Jack R." and the alteration by affidavit on October 23, 1947 to "John Hurd" comes from Ancestry.com.

CHAPTER TWO

Hone Connery's move to Florida in order to escape cold winters comes from ENG, as does the description of the cottage and workshop, and other family insights, such as the present of a fishing rod and reel from Hone to Jack. The Orange County Property Appraisal records have deed 19200202485 of March 19, 1920 for the land purchase of part of section 23 22 29 by Connery.

The Chattanooga photographic business was eventually sold to Basley Englerth ("Connery Photo Supply Company Changes Hands," *Chattanooga Daily Times*, October 24, 1920) and rebranded as the Englerth Photo Supply Company, shortened to Englerth's. It served the photographic needs in the Chattanooga area for many years ("Remembering Englerth's – Everything Photographic," by Harmon Jolley, November 29, 2011, https://www.chattanoogan.com/2011/11/29/214395/Remembering-Englerth-s---Everything.aspx).

The call for boys in the Orlando region to join the Boys Scout movement under scoutmaster Oscar Baynard appeared in the *Orlando Sentinel*, August 13, 1922. Baynard was an active scoutmaster in Plant City (*The Tampa Times*, October 19, 1921) before coming to Orlando and appointed deputy commissioner for Central Florida (*Orlando Sentinel*, July 22, 1923).

Jack rose quickly through the scout ranks in terms of merit badges ("Court of Honor Tonight," *Orlando Sentinel*, October 26, 1923), Life and Star badges ("Court of Honor," *Orlando Sentinel*, November 26, 1923), culminating in the Eagle Scout Award ("Court of Honor," *Orlando Sentinel*, February 16, 1924).

The summer scout camp was held at Silver Lake, initially in 1922 where Jack met Theodore Mead for the first time, and again in 1923 ("Scout Camp to be Opened Today," *Orlando Sentinel*, August 26, 1923). Jack winning the 'fire by friction' contest is documented in "Many Counties Attend Scouts' Rally Day Here," *Orlando Sentinel*, June 6, 1924. Camp Wewa became the permanent site in 1925, reached by taking the intersection of Boy Scout Blvd and the Old Dixie Hwy in Plymouth southwards (http://www.geocities.ws/krdvry/hikeplans/

plymouth/planplymouth.html). It was owned and operated by the Council of the Boy Scouts of America from 1925 to 1950, then passed into ownership of the Central Florida YMCA, and now belongs to the City of Apopka. Details of the 1925 camp come from "Many Boy Scouts Enter First Annual Campment, Plymouth," *Orlando Sentinel*, August 2, 1925, and the camp motto of 'every scout a swimmer' from "Flag Raising Program at Scout Camp," *Orlando Sentinel*, August 3, 1925. The bird trail created by Jack and the other Eagle scouts is described in "Eagle Scouts Make Trail at Scout Camp," *Orlando Sentinel*, July 19, 1925.

The 1926 improvements and new facilities appear in "Scout Headquarters Preparing for Annual Encampment Opens in June," *Orlando Sentinel*, May 30, 1926 and the accolade in "Camp Wewa – the Boy Scouts Paradise," *Orlando Sentinel*, August 15, 1926.

"Court of Honor Tonight," *Orlando Sentinel*, October 26, 1923 records Carl Dann Jr.'s scout membership of Troop 1, Orlando. His father's golf course, Dubsdread, derives its name from the intent of instilling dread in novice golfers, or "dubs". Members of the Orlando high school golf team, with Dann as captain, are documented in "High School will enter Golf Play," *Orlando Sentinel*, January 12, 1928. Dann took over from his father running the golf course and he and the rest of the Dann family operated it until it was taken over by the City of Orlando in 1978.

Henry Segrave was at Daytona Beach in March 1929 with his Irving Napier car, popularly known as the Golden Arrow. After a two-week delay caused by bad weather, and in front of an estimated crowd in excess of 100,000, he set a new world land speed of 231.45 mph. This was beaten by Malcolm Campbell in March 1931 driving Bluebird at Daytona Beach and recording 246.575 mph.

CHAPTER THREE

In 1912, Oscar E. Baynard was curator of birds for the Florida State Museum, Gainesville, now the Florida Museum of Natural History ("Audubon Society in Fort Myers," *Orlando Evening Star*, December 28, 1912). Gathering in the lakeside

Maitland home of Clara and Louis Dommerich, fifteen men and women—the "Who's Who" of Central Florida—agreed on March 2, 1900 to create the Florida Audubon Society, a statewide arm of the national Audubon movement. They pledged to protect birds that were being killed by the hundreds of thousands to supply plumes to adorn ladies' hats (Orange County History Center's, *Reflection Magazine*, September 2017). More information on the Society's founding and the then current senseless killing of birds for their feathers comes from "Feathered Friends," by Leslie Kemp Poole in *Winter Park Magazine,* Winter 2018.

The description of Bird Island appears in "Report of P. B. Philipp on Bird Island, Orange Lake, Florida, 1911," in *Bird-Lore*, vol. XIII, no. 6, pp. 358-362 (1911). The article refers to a bird population of approximately 10,000 pairs. News of Baynard's purchase of Bird Island on behalf of the National Association of Florida Societies is contained in *The Oologist*, vol. XXVIII, no. 6, p. 11 (1911). With the protection of an Audubon warden to deter plume hunters at Bird Island, Baynard claim that Alachua County had more egrets than any other state in Florida comes from "A History of Birding in Alachua County," by Rex Rowan, https://www.alachuaaudubon.org/our-community/history.

News of Baynard's Christmas cruise of the Keys, accompanied by W. F. Blackman and Herbert R. Mills, is from "Audubon Society in Fort Myers," *Orlando Evening Star*, December 28, 1912, and the full list of bird species spotted over Christmas Day, 7 a.m. to 5 p.m., was reported in *Bird-Lore*, vol. XV, no. 1, p. 33 (1913). A copy of the photograph of W. F. Blackman holding eaglets, taken by Baynard, appears in *The Oologist*, vol. XXXIII, no. 1, p. 27 (1916). William Freeman Blackman, was Rollins fourth president from 1902 to 1915, and a dedicated bird lover and conservationist, joining the Florida Audubon Society upon his arrival in Winter Park. The article "Photographing Birds' Nests," by Oscar E. Baynard, was published in *Bird-Lore*, vol. XVI, no. 6. pp. 471-477 (1914).

The photograph of the nest and eggs of the Florida Bobwhite taken by Jack Connery on April 25, 1925 was used in the article "Life Histories of North American Gallinaceous Birds," by Arthur Cleveland Bent, United States National

Museum Bulletin, 162, plate 5, Smithsonian Institution, Washington D. C. (1932). The Baynard comment that "Most all birds will repeat their laying after the eggs are removed from the nest" is stated in "This Ornithologist really hates those Bird Hunters," *The Tampa Times*, December 19, 1960. His claim to have climbed more than a thousand trees in his lifetime of egg-hunting also appears in this reference.

Jack Connery and Oscar Baynard's exploration of the Kissimmee rookery is reported in "Jack Connery finds Rookery: Strange Creatures arise by Hundreds on Approach of Strangers," *Orlando Evening Star*, May 3, 1931. Baynard's bald eagle hunts in Florida, including his Christmas Eve bivouac, are described in "The Bald Eagle in Florida," by Oscar Baynard, *The Oologist,* vol. XXXIII, no. 2, pp. 17-21 (1916). The comment "Just for the fun of it" is taken from "1,500-Egg Exhibit Given Museum," *St. Petersburg Times*, July 11, 1959.

"Scouts Bid Farewell to Rollins Leaders," *Orlando Sentinel*, February 7, 1935 records Joe Howell's leadership of the Winter Park Pathfinder Troop. He stayed with ornithology and made a successful academic career of it. From Rollins College, he studied zoology for a doctorate at Cornell University, then through several academic institutions ending as Professor of Zoology in the Department of Zoology and Entomology at the University of Tennessee, Knoxville. He retained a keen interest in the bald eagles of Florida, writing several articles relating to their nest sites and population variances over the 1930s to 1950s. His tree fall made the newspapers in "Youth is Injured in Fall from Tree," *Orlando Sentinel*, December 4, 1928.

Baynard's move to become a poultry farmer in Plant City is reported in "Cost of Egg Production cut to Minimum at Baywood," *Plant City Courier*, March 8, 1929. His efforts at Highlands Hammock to document all bird species on Christmas Day 1937 is documented in "Highlands Hammock," by Allen Altvater, p. 57, https://www.allenaltvater.org/HighlandsHammock.htm. As superintendent of the Hillsborough River State Park, his legacy lives on through the park's 2.2-mile

Baynard Trail. The gift of his entire egg collection appears as "1,500-Egg Exhibit Given Museum," *St. Petersburg Times*, July 11, 1959.

Jack's statement about the fascination of bird study comes from the article "Young Florida Naturalist Tells of his Bird Study," *Orlando Evening Star*, May 3, 1931.

CHAPTER FOUR

The reader is referred to the book by Gould for more details of the life and times of William Beebe.

The Liberty Street clubhouse of the Orlando chapter of Sorosis opened in 1922, and the program for December 8, 1925 featured "The Life and Work of William Beebe," and a review of the Galapagos book ("Literature Day at Sorosis Yesterday," *Orlando Sentinel*, December 9, 1925). The impact this event had, and his stated desire to join one of Beebe's expeditions, was recalled by Jack in "Jack Connery Tells of Bermuda Exploits," *Orlando Sentinel*, April 12, 1931.

Beebe was Curator of Birds for the New York Zoological Park and brought back many collections on his travels (William Beebe, George Inness Hartley, and Paul Griswold Howes, *Tropical Wild Life in British Guiana* (New York: New York Zoological Society, 1917). The New York Zoological Society is now the Wildlife Conservation Society (WCS) and the New York Zoological Park is now the Bronx Zoo.

Professor William Gregory's experience of helmet diving with Beebe in the Sargasso Sea was described in "Down to the Sea in Ships," *The Brooklyn Daily Eagle*, November 1, 1925. Beebe used the technique on his first Nonsuch Island expedition in 1929 ("Dr. Beebe Studies World under Sea from Workshop on Bermuda Shore," *The Boston Globe*, October 4, 1929). The privileged few that had experienced these fascinating walks at the bottom of the sea in the 'Kingdom of the Helmet' were enrolled by Beebe as members of the 'Society of Wonderers' (*Half Mile Down*, p. 86).

Otis Barton was a wealthy single Harvard graduate also with a passion for exploration and adventure. He had an engineering background and was attending postgraduate studies at Columbia University. Besides having a restless spirit similar to Beebe, Barton also had in his hands a substantial amount of money that he inherited from his grandfather.

Jack Connery's meeting with Beebe about joining his expedition appear in "Jack Connery Tells of Bermuda Exploits," *Orlando Sentinel*, April 12, 1931.

CHAPTER FIVE

The arrival of the Beebe's party in Bermuda is captured in "Dr. Beebe Arrives," *The Royal Gazette and Colonist Daily*, April 12, 1930, and also in "The Beebe Lecture," *The Royal Gazette and Colonist Daily*, April 14, 1930. Else Bostelman was hired to be the principal expedition artist and she rendered over 300 plates of deep-sea and shore fish, including the giant squid (krakan). The part she played in the history of deep-sea exploration is celebrated in "The Fine Art of Exploration" by Edith Widder, *Oceanography*, vol. 29, no. 4, pp. 170-177 (2016), accessed via https://doi.org/10.5670/oceanog.2016.86.

The process of net trawling is described in "Bermuda Oceanographic Expeditions 1929-1930," *Zoologica*, vol. XIII, no. I, 1931, and in "Jack Connery Tells of Bermuda Exploits," *Orlando Sentinel*, April 12, 1931. This latter reference also contains an account of Jack's thrilling experience of helmet diving and walking on the seabed. The arrival of William Gregory and Jocelyn Crane is mentioned in Matsen, p. 101.

Gould's book, pp. 296-298, describes some of the parties that Beebe organized to lift flagging spirits of his team, including the birthday celebration one in July 1930 that had a pirate theme.

CHAPTER SIX

An account of the May bathysphere test dives in St. George's harbor comes from Gould, p. 282 and the June deep-sea ones from Matsen, pp. 69-76. Jack Connery tripping the shutter before the first record breaking descent can be found in Matsen, p. 79-80. Beebe's impressions at the start of the descent are recorded in *Half Mile Down*, p. 118, and his comment "the most vivid experience in life" is taken from *The Eternal Darkness*, p. 13.

Although marine detritus was postulated in the late 19th century as a source of food for seafloor life, Beebe was the first to directly observe it and term it 'marine snow', see "Marine Snow: A Brief Historical Sketch" by Mary Silver, *Limnology and Oceanography Bulletin*, vol. 24, no. 1, pp. 5-10 (2015).

The record of Jack's accident where he injured his back is in Matsen, p. 102. Hollister's method of revealing the skeletal structures of fish was published as "Cleaning and Dyeing Fish for Bone Study" by Gloria Hollister, *Zoologica*, vol. 12, no. 10, pp. 89-101 (1934). Jackson Patten's tragic death is covered in Gould's book, p. 302.

CHAPTER SEVEN

Jack Connery's Bermuda talks are documented at the scouts ("Scouts to Hear of Deep-Sea Adventure," *Orlando Sentinel*, April 24, 1931) and at the Junior Chamber of Commerce ("Naturalist to Speak at Chamber Monday," *Orlando Evening Star*, September 13, 1931). Newspaper coverage appears as "Jack Connery Tells of Bermuda Exploits," *Orlando Sentinel*, April 12, 1931.

Audubon-related presentations include "Hold Audubon Entertainment," *Orlando Sentinel*, April 15, 1931, and his plead to school children to shoot birds only with a camera was delivered in "Jack Connery gives lecture at school," *Orlando Sentinel*, February 27, 1932. His transformative experience of a rookery led to him arrange a visit for school clubs to one on a bird island near Port Orange ("Connery Arranges Bird Trip for School Clubs," *Orlando Evening Star*, June 21,

1931). Dann, the golfer, spoke to the Florida Audubon Society using plenty of references to 'birdies' and 'eagles' ("Carl Dann to Talk on Birdies, Eagles at Audubon Society," *Orlando Sentinel*, March 8, 1930). The newspaper piece that Connery wrote extolling the virtues of the natural world is "Pencil Made up of Many Natural Things," *Orlando Sentinel*, October 14, 1928.

"The Making of a Botanical Garden" by Edwin Grover (*Parks & Recreation*, August 1948, p. 450) documents Connery's appointment as museum curator and his promise to build a memorial garden in honor of Theodore Mead. A lecture on bird life in Florida, to be given to Rollins' biology students by Jack Connery as "Instructor of Ornithology," is mentioned in *Sandspur*, vol. 37, no. 2. October 12, 1932.

Letters from Theodore Mead to the Willis family record the Connerys taking him to Daytona Beach on Independence Day (Letter Mead to Ogden Willis, Oviedo, July 5, 1932, WC) and celebrating his 81st birthday (Letter Mead to Willis family, Oviedo, February 24, 1933, WC).

The Rollins Alumni Record, vol. XII, September 1935, p. 4 and *The Rollins Alumni Record*, vol. XXVI, September 1948, p. 14 documents Iverne Galloway's career as a children's author and pen name of Elizabeth Ireland. Jack and Helen's engagement notice appeared in the *Orlando Evening Star*, June 19, 1932. Helen's impressions of the parlor at Mead's home comes from an unpublished text in RC-TLM, written by Helen Golloway.

The Rollins College request to excavate at Kelly Park is reported in the *Orlando Evening Star*, November 2, 1931, and *The Rollins Alumni Record* of December 1931, p. 9, states it would require John Hopkins University to agree to any digging. In the February 11, 1932, issue of *The Flagler Tribune* it was noted that Ed Johnson had made arrangements with Rollins College to make extensive excavations at the Bon Terra site. Members of the Flagler Beach party on the first successful dig were mentioned in a footnote to Connery's *Science* article; "Recent Find of Mammoth remains in the Quaternary of Florida, together with Arrowhead," Jack H. Connery, *Science*, vol. 75, no. 1950, p. 516 (May

13, 1932). The footnote reads: "A professor, Dr. Frank Guy Armitage, six students, Harold Cochenour, Guilford Galbraith, Daniel Havens, Robert Maclay, Douglas Riggs, and Jack Connery, and one visitor, Kenneth Wooldridge." Dr. Frank Guy Armitage was a visiting instructor at Rollins College and an expert on the books of Dickens. He was well-known for his animated talks on Dickens' characters whom Armitage impersonated via their speech, mannerisms and dress.

Despite superficial resemblances, mammoths were distinct from mastodons. Mastodons were shorter and stockier than mammoths with shorter, straighter tusks, and their molars had pointed cones specially adapted for eating twigs, buds, and leaves of trees and shrubs. Mammoths were grazers so their molars had flat surfaces for eating grass.

The belief that humans were not in Florida early enough to interact with mammoths persisted for many years in the form of the Clovis-first theory; see https://en.wikipedia.org/wiki/Clovis_culture. This entrenched philosophy is now commonly questioned, for example, Smith, Morgan F. "A Mammoth Question," *2020 Adventures in Florida Archaeology,* Florida Historical Society Archaeological Institute, pp. 50-58. Newspapers had no such problems in making the man-mammoth connection, "Arrowhead Found in Skull Shows Man and Mammoth Lived Together in Florida," *The Evening Independent*, St. Petersburg, Florida, May 7, 1932.

Rollins College student Carrington Lloyd was a key supporter of Jack Connery's work for the museum and the work they did together excavating Indian mounds was published in *Sandspur*, vol. 37, no. 6, November 9, 1932. The donation of $1,000 to continue fossil hunting, approximately $15,000 at today's (2020) valuation, came from an unknown donor (*Sandspur*, vol. 37 no. 11, December 14, 1932, and "Rollins Gets $1000 for Excavations," *Orlando Evening Star*, December 9, 1932), later revealed to be Lloyd's mother. Hanna's note to Hamilton Holt in is the Explorers Club files of Rollins College archives. Impressed by Jack's Bermuda expedition with William Beebe, Lloyd and his family helped support

Beebe's twenty-second expedition tour of the islands of the West Indies, January – March, 1936 ("A West Indian Grand Tour," *The Royal Gazette and Colonist Daily*, November 7, 1936, p. 3). The second dig at Flagler Beach comes from *Sandspur*, vol. 37, no. 12, January 4, 1933. "Explorers Club Organizes Trip to Saber Tooth Cave," appears in *Sandspur*, vol. 37, no. 16, February 1, 1933.

A letter from Jack Connery to A. C. Altvater dated February 2, 1940 (Explorers Club files of Rollins College archives), details his presence there in 1932 and 1933 and the excavation and extraction of the fossilized turtle. More information can be found in "Highlands Hammock" by Allen Altvater, https://www.allenaltvater.org/HighlandsHammock.htm. The Seminole Indian's presence there is documented as "Indians to Act in Hammock Pageant," *The Tampa Tribune*, March 6, 1933, and "Pageants Will be Given at Highlands Hammock," *The Tampa Tribune*, March 15, 1933. The appointment of Edward Davies as the new Baker Museum director was recorded in the *Rollins Alumni Record*, vol. XI, no. 3, September 1934, p. 2. The proposed move of the museum to the Aloma Golf Clubhouse features with photograph on the front page of *Winter Park Topics*, vol. 7, no. 4, January 20, 1940.

Neill's reevaluation of the Flagler Beach investigation and conclusions appeared as "Notes on the Supposed Association of Artifacts and Extinct Vertebrates in Flagler County, Florida," by Wilfred T. Neill and I. Rouse, *American Antiquity*, 19 (2): pp. 170-171, 1953. Many articles now debunk the Clovis-first hypothesis, such as https://arstechnica.com/science/2017/11/majority-of-scientists-now-agree-that-humans-came-to-the-americas-by-boat, but Hoffman's 1983 paper was one of the first to be taken seriously (Hoffman, Charles A. "A Mammoth Kill Site in the Silver Springs Run," *The Florida Anthropologist*, 36(1-2), pp. 83-87). The letter from Hoffman to the Rollins College president dated January 17, 2000 is in the Rollins College archives, as are the three relevant pages of the manuscript praising Connery's work that Hoffman was preparing for publication.

CHAPTER EIGHT

Marriage reports for the weddings of Connery/Golloway and Palmer/Brogden are in the *Orlando Sentinel* of June 1, 1934 and September 13, 1935, respectively. The Brogden citrus fruit patent is E. M. Brogden and M. L. Trowbridge, "Preparation of fresh fruit for market," US Patent US1903283A, 1933. Details of Mead's funeral service are contained in *Orchids and Butterflies* p. 283.

Mead's original orchid donation to the Royal Palm State Park is documented in letters dated September 18, 1916 and February 9, 1918 from W. S. Jennings to T. L. Mead (RC-TLM). The 'blooming treasure' comment graces a headline in *The Miami News*, March 6. 1938, p. 15. Attempts to acquire Mead's Oviedo estate by Orange County and Rollins College can be found in the *Orlando Sentinel*, June 6, 1936, and a letter from Grover to Willis dated January 6, 1937 (RC-TLM), respectively. Jack Connery seemed certain in a letter dated August 13, 1936 to Mr. and Mrs. Hunter (RC-TLM) that the memorial garden would be in Orlando.

The Connery's meeting with Edwin Grover, their trip into the proposed site with the rookery, and the WPA activities surrounding the building of Mead Botanical Garden are described in *Hope Springs Eternal*. The practicality of using sea water in an inland aquarium was explained in the *Orlando Sentinel*, June 16, 1938. Jack's use of armed guards to protect his plants is documented in "How they built Mead" by Martin Andersen, the *Orlando Sentinel*, September 19, 1939.

The events on the official groundbreaking day are recorded in the *Orlando Sentinel*, January 8, 1938. "For nine years Jack cherished this dream," comes from the *Orlando Evening Star*, January 9, 1938. Andersen's question as to who was responsible for the garden was reported in "Dr. Grover Tells his Tale," *Orlando Sentinel*, June 30, 1961. Jack's popularity with the WPA workers features in "They Call Him Jack," *St. Petersburg Times*, March 4, 1939. The report of the baptism of infant Edwin with Grover as godfather can be found in the *Rollins Alumni Record*, June 1938, p. 3.

"Transplanted nearly a thousand (palms)" is a statement Grover made about Jack's particular skill in that area ("The History of Mead Botanical Garden," an undated but probably early 1960s manuscript by Grover in RC-TLM). John A. Porter's death was reported in "Orlando the Loser," *Orlando Sentinel*, April 25, 1939, and the opportunity to acquire the greenhouse comes from a letter from Helen Connery to Mrs. Sprague-Smith, dated May 28, 1939 (RC-TLM). "Now's the Opportunity" was how one appeal by Martin Andersen to his readers ended (*Orlando Sentinel*, November 5, 1939). A grateful Grover replied to this urging in a letter dated November 15, 1939, RC-TLM.

Opening day was extensively covered in "Hundreds Stroll Thru Mead Garden on Opening Day," *Orlando Sentinel*, January 15, 1940. Planting the Bartram tree was reported as "Mead Garden Prepares New Plantings," *Orlando Sentinel*, February 12, 1939, and the scouts planting an evergreen in the *Orlando Sentinel*, January 31, 1940. An example of Helen Connery's writing appeared as "Creating a Tropical Wonderland," in *Subtropical Gardening*, November 1938. The report of Graham Grover's funeral was covered as "Grover Funeral to be Held Today," *Orlando Sentinel*, March 6, 1940.

CHAPTER NINE

Plat number 1922P00G107 is from the Orange County Comptroller website (http://or.occompt.com/recorder/eagleweb/docSearch.jsp) and shows the Connery purchase as lots 1 and 2 of block L, Virginia Heights; lots that are now classified as being part of Stirling Avenue (numbers 300 and 320). Moving into the new house is documented in the *Orlando Sentinel*, September 23, 1941. Jack's entry to Mead Garden from the house via the Dinky Line, and Helen's doctor advising Jack to secure a proper are both from a private communication with Edwin Connery. Helen's appointment as personal secretary to Dr. Edwin Grover, then Vice-President of Rollins College, is contained in a letter from Helen Connery to Donna Rhein, July 15, 1995, WPPL.

The cow pasture reference for the airbase site appears in the *Orlando Sentinel*, April 6, 1942, and details of the site plan in "Details of New Orlando Air Base show 57 buildings in Plan," *Orlando Sentinel*, July 10, 1940. The award of the WPA grant is recorded in the *Orlando Evening Star*, July 22, 1940, and commencement of the project in the *Orlando Sentinel*, March 18, 1941. "16,000 More Palm Trees set out at Air Base," comes from the *Orlando Evening Star*, April 24, 1941. The National Youth Administration (NYA) focused on providing work and education for Americans between the ages of 16 and 25. It operated from 1935 to 1939 as part of the Works Progress Administration (WPA) and was then transferred to the Federal Security Agency (FSA), aimed at training people for jobs in war industries. Recognition of Jack's contribution to the airbase project form part of "Amazing Transformation Made in Orlando Air Base," *Orlando Sentinel*, April 6, 1942. Excavation of peat from the Mead Botanical Garden site is described in "Dr. Grover Tells his Tale," *Orlando Evening Star*, June 30, 1961. Construction of the lily ponds comes from the *Orlando Evening Star*, August 9, 1942.

The move to vegetable production at Zellwood is described in "Vegetable Production at Zellwood," by R. S. Dowdell, Florida State Horticultural Society, 1944, pp. 221-224; and "Corncob Jack" in the *Orlando Evening Star*, August 18, 1944. The giant vegetables grown at Zellwood feature in a story in the *Orlando Evening Star*, May 5, 1944. Dr. Brown Landone, founder of the Brown Landone foundation and author of several hundred booklets and pamphlets, was a key promoter of ramie as a new wonder crop for Florida (*The Key West Citizen*, November 21, 1942). He died at his home in Winter Park, Florida, aged 97, in October, 1945 (*Tampa Bay Times*, October 21, 1945). The story of the letter from Grover to Holt containing ramie fiber and the challenge to see if Holt could break it appears in *The Business of Making Good*, p. 79.

Jack's appointment as scoutmaster is documented in the *Orlando Sentinel*, December 30, 1938, and the scout meetings at his Lake Worth home in *The Palm Beach Post*, May 11, 1945 and February 17, 1946. The progress of his two sons in the Cub Scouts comes from *The Palm Beach Post*, October 18, 1947. Reports of the Sea Scouts visit to the Coast Guard station can be found in *The Miami News*, July 1, 1945, and the Sunday cruise at *The Palm Beach Post*, April 9, 1946. Jack's successful use of a chemical spray to control water hyacinth is reported in *The Palm Beach Post*, March 30, 1946, and his presentation to the authorities in *The Miami News*, April 14, 1946. The invasive weed covered more than 120,000 acres of public lakes and navigable rivers by the early 1960s, and remains difficult to control. Recently, however, it has been discovered to be beneficial in ridding waters of contaminants and heavy metals.

Cuba had a strategic interest in growing ramie to help diversify their agriculture ("Cuba Looks to Industry from Fiber," *The Miami Herald*, September 6, 1953). Unfortunately, and unknown to Jack, Aleman was a highly unsavory character, described by Fulgencio Batista on page 80 of his book "The Growth and Decline of the Cuban Republic" (The Devin-Adair Company, New York, 1964) as a "prodigious thief". On his relatively modest salary as a Cuban minister, he managed to buy assets worth millions of dollars in the Miami area (*The Miami News*, March 25, 1950). The contract with the Aleman organization was an oral one with a salary of $7,000 (approximately $80,000 in 2021 terms) for five years (*The Miami Herald*, January 16, 1951). The hurricane damage at Belle Glade is described in *The Tampa Tribune*, August 28, 1949, and the plan for the site to be taken over by the state in *The Bradenton Herald*, September 23, 1949. Documentation of Jack's visit to the King Ranch in Texas to purchase Santa Gertrudis cattle for Aleman can be found in *The Business of Making Good*, p. 79. Helen's activities with the Havana Woman's Club appears in *The Miami Herald*, February 21, 1951.

Aleman's death was widely reported, for example: *The Miami News*, March 25, 1950; *The Palm Beach Post*, March 26, 1950; and *The Bradenton Herald*, March 26, 1950. Jack's attempt to sue for wrongful dismissal comes from *The Miami Herald*, January 16, 1951.

CHAPTER TEN

Joe Connery and his wife Rena's presence in DeLand comes from entries in the appropriate US City Directories for that time. How Helen Connery acquired the nickname "Mimi" can be found in the *Orlando Sentinel*, November 13, 1955. Her positions as flower show chairman and president of the Deland Garden Club appear in the *Orlando Sentinel* on October 23, 1952; October 15, 1954; and February 25, 1955. Jack Connery was head of the Deland horticultural show committee in 1953 (*Orlando Sentinel*, October 14, 1953). In 1953, a massive and costly renovation created a water-themed attraction park surrounding the Ponce de Leon Springs (*Journal of Florida Studies*, vol. 1, no. 6, 2017), becoming one of many roadside attractions claiming the title, "The Fountain of Youth." It was complete with a statue of a conquistador (Rick Kilby, "Finding the Fountain of Youth," University of Florida Press, 2013). Jack was in charge of landscaping and lush tropical planting around the areas of the jungle cruise (*Orlando Sentinel*, May 30, 1953).

Connery and Grover signing their waivers on the money they had advanced the Garden is covered in the *Orlando Sentinel*, December 17, 1952 and the *Orlando Evening Star*, December 18, 1952. Helping to clear up the Garden is from the *Orlando Sentinel*, November 5, 1953, and Edwin's lunch experiences were captured in a private communication (EC). The hibiscus show at Mead Botanical Garden was on Sunday, June 24, 1951 (*Orlando Evening Star*, June 23, 1951). Suzy Johnson's hibiscus hybrid awards appear in the *Orlando Sentinel*, July 22, 1956 and September 9, 1957, and Steven Johnson's in the September 26, 1960 edition. The Johnson's hibiscus experiences and the devastating cold that ended their enthusiasm for the flower is documented in the *Orlando Sentinel*, August 14, 1982.

The reasons behind the bursting of the ramie boom were covered in *The Tampa Tribune*, November 29, 1951. "DeLand Man Plans Wealth from Kenaf," headlines an article in the *Orlando Evening Star*, August 4, 1952. Jack's tendency to occasionally exaggerate was commented on by Grover ("The History of the Mead Botanical Garden," by Edwin Grover, unpublished manuscript, circa 1960, RC-TLM). The disasters affecting initial kenaf seed growing were the subject of *The Miami News* article on May 24, 1953.

Details of liquidating the stock of the Silver Springs Nursery and the balance transferred to Mimi's Nursery are reported in the *Ocala Star Banner*, April 28 and May 22, 1955. A record of Jack operating the Ocala Garden Mart is found in the *Ocala Star Banner*, September 21, 1956. Both Jack and Helen gave gardening talks; Jack on growing annuals (*Orlando Sentinel*, September 21, 1955) and Helen on growing African violets (*Orlando Sentinel*, April 7, 1956). By this time, Helen had more than 10,000 violets in her collection (*Orlando Sentinel*, November 13, 1955) and was in demand, often assisted by Jack, to give expert classes on their culture; for example as reported in the *Orlando Sentinel*, January 14, 1959, and the AVM, vol. 21, September 1968, p. 44. Helen's landscaping design award appears in *The Miami News*, April 4, 1957, p. 26.

CHAPTER ELEVEN

Details of the 1956 Tropical Storm Ten that hit DeLand can be found at en.wikipedia.org/wiki/1956_Atlantic_hurricane_season, and the award of a disaster loan in the document "10th Semiannual Small Business Administration for six months ending June 30, 1958," Appendix G – Disaster Loans Approved, p. 199.

The *Fort Lauderdale News* of June 21, 1962, advertised the Connery's presence at Woolworth stores in Pompano Beach and Fort Lauderdale. The DeLand City Directory of 1960 refers to Jack's sons as assistant managers to the African violet business. Dicks' research into the effects of artificial light on the growth of African violets appeared in the AVM, vol. 21, June 1968, p. 16; vol. 21. September 1968, p. 42; vol. 22, November 1968, p. 42; vol. 22, January 1969, p. 66; and vol. 22, March 1969, p. 33. The *Hattiesburg American* of August 5, 1965 recorded one of their first out-of-state events. In April 1966 the Connerys attended the Miami Beach convention (AVM, vol. 19, June 1966, p. 57) and were voted "most cooperative" of all the commercial growers there (AVM, vol. 20, September 1966, p. 21). At the 1967 Miami show they received an award of distinction for their "Pathways to Beauty" display (AVM, vol. 21, November 1967, p. 9). One example of their many visits to Tennessee appears in the *Johnson City Press*, June 28, 1967. More accolades followed at the February 1969 show in Miami where they were awarded best commercial display (AVM, vol. 22, June 1969, p. 33). In September 1969 they attended the convention in Baton Rouge and gave each attendees a gift of their new cultivar "Miss Baton Rouge" (AVM, vol. 22, September 1969, p. 43).

The last date found for a Connery African violet clinic has been in the *Fort Lauderdale News*, October 12, 1972. Tours of Mimi's nursery continued, and several were reported, for example (AVM, vol. 26, September 1973, p. 45; *Panama City News Herald*, November 11, 1973; *Tampa Bay Times*, October 12, 1976; *Orlando Sentinel*, February 11, 1979). Mimi's African violet starter kits were being sold both in Woolworth and mail-order (*Orlando Sentinel*, April 30, 1976; AVM, vol. 29, November 1976). By this time Suzy Johnson had become active in the African violet scene, giving talks on their care and culture (*Orlando Sentinel*, March 16, 1969; *Orlando Evening Star*, March 21, 1972), and in 1968 she founded and became club president of the Haines City African Violet Society (AVM, vol. 22, November 1968, p. 61), and eventually established in 1971 the Central Florida African Violet Society ("Finally, we made it!" AVM, vol. 24, November 1971, p. 26).

CHAPTER TWELVE

"Lived life with exuberance" is from the ENG manuscript and recalls a comment made by one of Jack's aunts with regard to his philosophy to life. Jack's energy, enthusiasm and happy disposition was commented on in "They Call Him Jack," *St. Petersburg Times*, March 4, 1939.

The durable power of attorney was signed on July 18, 1978 (Orange County Comptroller, POA 19781265253, Book 2913, Page 1160).

Jack Connery's palm trees can be seen at the Winter Park entrance to Mead Botanical Garden but also in the area around Festival Park in Orlando which used to be part of the site of the Orlando Air Base.

Picture Credits

T = top, B = bottom, L = left, R = right, TR = top right, TL = top left, BR = bottom right, BL = bottom left.

Cover: The Boomslang aerial tree canopy walkway at Kirstenbosch National Botanical Gardens, Cape Town, South Africa. Photograph by Adam Harrower and used with permission.

Frontispiece, 1.1B, 2.3, 2.5, 3.3L, 3.3R, 3.4, 3.5TL, 3.5TR, 3.5B, 5.2, 5.4M, 5.4B, 5.5T, 5.5BL, 5.5BM, 5.5BR, 6.1T, 6.1M, 6.1B, 6.2, 6.3, 6.4, 7.2L, 7.2R, 7.3, 7.4, 7.5, 7.6, 7.8, 7.9, 8.1, 8.2TL, 8.2TR, 8.2BL, 8.2BR, 8.4, 8.5, 8.8, 9.1, 9.4, 9.5, 10.1T, 10.1B, 10.5, 11.4, 12.1, 12.2: Courtesy of the Edwin Connery and family collections.

1.1T: From the Science Museum Group collection. Creative Commons BY-NC-SA.

1.2: From Ancestry.com.

2.1: From the Orlando Sentinel, March 6, 1927, p. 12.

2.2L: From The Oologist, vol. XXVIII, no. 6, June 1911.

2.2R: From http://www.eaglescoutbadge.com/badges_robbins.html.

2.4: From Senior Class: Orlando High School, "Las Memorias, 1928," p. 123, https://stars.library.ucf/cfm-texts/473.

3.1: Postcard from the Matheson History Museum collection, Gainesville, Florida.

3.2: Photograph by Oscar Baynard from The Oologist, vol. XXXIII, no. 1, p. 27 (1916).

4.1: From Elswyth Thane Collection, Howard Gotlieb Archival Research Center, Boston University.

4.2: From Heritage Auctions, www.HA.com.

4.3: From "The Arcturus Adventure" by William Beebe, p. 88, G. P. Putnam's Sons, New York, The Knickerbocker Press (1926).

4.4: From Charles Riddiford/National Geographic Society Image Collection.

5.1: From the archives of the National Geographic.

5.3: From Zoologica, vol. XIII, no. 1, p. 2, 1931.

5.4TL: From Zoologica, vol. XIII, no. 1, p. 9, 1931.

7.1: Courtesy of the Willis family collection.

7.7: From https://www.floridastateparks.org/learn/finding-objects-ice-age.

8.3, 8.6, 8.7: From the Winter Park Garden Club Collection, Archives & Special Collections, Rollins College, Winter Park, Florida.

9.2: Postcard taken 1942 by Thomas Pickett Robinson, Historical Society of Central Florida, Inc.

9.3: From https://www.newthoughtwisdom.com/browne-landone.html.

9.6: Postcard by the Curt Teich Company, Chicago.

10.2L: From the De Leon Springs Museum collection.

10.2R: From "Finding the fountain of youth" by Rick Kilby, p. 74.

10.3: Star photo by Ralph Ward from the Orlando Evening Star, September 6, 1957, p. 6.

10.4: From the Orlando Sentinel, October 27, 1957.

11.1: From "Cultural Guidelines for Commercial Production of African Violets (*Saintpaulia Ionantha*)" by J. Chen and R. J. Henny, Publication #ENH 1096, Environmental Horticulture Department, University of Florida (2018).

11.2: From the personal collection of Eduard Gfeller.

11.3: From newspapers.com.

11.5: Open access to the African Violet magazine via the Biodiversity Heritage Library.

12.3: Author's collection.

ALSO BY PAUL BUTLER